MAX LUCADO

LIFE LESSONS *from*
LUKE

Jesus, the Son of Man

PREPARED BY THE LIVINGSTONE CORPORATION

THOMAS NELSON
Since 1798

Life Lessons from Luke

© 2018 by Max Lucado

Published in Nashville, Tennessee, by Thomas Nelson. Thomas Nelson is a registered trademark of HarperCollins Christian Publishing, Inc.

Produced with the assistance of the Livingstone Corporation (www.livingstonecorp.com). Project staff includes Jake Barton, Joel Bartlett, Andy Culbertson, Mary Horner Collins, and Will Reaves.

Editor: Neil Wilson

Material for the "Inspiration" sections taken from the following books:

And the Angels Were Silent. Copyright © 2004 by Max Lucado. Thomas Nelson, a registered trademark of HarperCollins Christian Publishing, Inc., Nashville, Tennessee.

Before Amen. Copyright © 2014 by Max Lucado. Thomas Nelson, a registered trademark of HarperCollins Christian Publishing, Inc., Nashville, Tennessee.

God Came Near. Copyright © 2004 by Max Lucado. Thomas Nelson, a registered trademark of HarperCollins Christian Publishing, Inc., Nashville, Tennessee.

The Great House of God. Copyright © 1997 by Max Lucado. Thomas Nelson, a registered trademark of HarperCollins Christian Publishing, Inc., Nashville, Tennessee.

He Still Moves Stones. Copyright © 1993 by Max Lucado. Thomas Nelson, a registered trademark of HarperCollins Christian Publishing, Inc., Nashville, Tennessee.

It's Not About Me. Copyright © 2004 by Max Lucado. Thomas Nelson, a registered trademark of HarperCollins Christian Publishing, Inc., Nashville, Tennessee.

Next Door Savior. Copyright © 2003 by Max Lucado. Thomas Nelson, a registered trademark of HarperCollins Christian Publishing, Inc., Nashville, Tennessee.

Shaped by God (previously published as *On the Anvil*). Copyright © 2001 by Max Lucado. Tyndale House Publishers, Carol Stream, Illinois.

Six Hours One Friday. Copyright © 2004 by Max Lucado. Thomas Nelson, a registered trademark of HarperCollins Christian Publishing, Inc., Nashville, Tennessee.

Thomas Nelson titles may be purchased in bulk for educational, business, fundraising, or sales promotional use. For information, please e-mail SpecialMarkets@ThomasNelson.com.

ISBN 978-0-310-08634-5

First Printing December 2017 / Printed in the United States of America

CONTENTS

HOW TO STUDY THE BIBLE

The Bible is a peculiar book. Words crafted in another language. Deeds done in a distant era. Events recorded in a far-off land. Counsel offered to a foreign people. It is a peculiar book.

It's surprising that anyone reads it. It's too old. Some of its writings date back 5,000 years. It's too bizarre. The book speaks of incredible floods, fires, earthquakes, and people with supernatural abilities. It's too radical. The Bible calls for undying devotion to a carpenter who called himself God's Son.

Logic says this book shouldn't survive. Too old, too bizarre, too radical.

The Bible has been banned, burned, scoffed, and ridiculed. Scholars have mocked it as foolish. Kings have branded it as illegal. A thousand times over the grave has been dug and the dirge has begun, but somehow the Bible never stays in the grave. Not only has it survived, but it has also thrived. It is the single most popular book in all of history. It has been the bestselling book in the world for years!

There is no way on earth to explain it. Which perhaps is the only explanation. For the Bible's durability is not found on *earth* but in *heaven*. The millions who have tested its claims and claimed its promises know there is but one answer: the Bible is God's book and God's voice.

As you read it, you would be wise to give some thought to two questions: *What is the purpose of the Bible?* and *How do I study the Bible?* Time spent reflecting on these two issues will greatly enhance your Bible study.

What is the purpose of the Bible?

Let the Bible itself answer that question: *"From infancy you have known the Holy Scriptures, which are able to make you wise for salvation through faith in Christ Jesus"* (2 Timothy 3:15).

The purpose of the Bible? Salvation. God's highest passion is to get his children home. His book, the Bible, describes his plan of salvation. The purpose of the Bible is to proclaim God's plan and passion to save his children.

This is the reason why this book has endured through the centuries. It dares to tackle the toughest questions about life: *Where do I go after I die? Is there a God? What do I do with my fears?* The Bible is the treasure map that leads to God's highest treasure—eternal life.

But how do you study the Bible? Countless copies of Scripture sit unread on bookshelves and nightstands simply because people don't know how to read it. What can you do to make the Bible real in your life?

The clearest answer is found in the words of Jesus: *"Ask and it will be given to you; seek and you will find; knock and the door will be opened to you"* (Matthew 7:7).

The first step in understanding the Bible is asking God to help you. Your should read it prayerfully. If anyone understands God's Word, it is because of God and not the reader.

"The Advocate, the Holy Spirit, whom the Father will send in my name, will teach you all things and will remind you of everything I have said to you" (John 14:26).

Before reading the Bible, pray and invite God to speak to you. Don't go to Scripture looking for your idea, but go searching for his.

Not only should you read the Bible prayerfully, but you should also read it carefully. *"Seek and you will find"* is the pledge. The Bible is not a newspaper to be skimmed but rather a mine to be quarried. *"If you look for it as for silver and search for it as for hidden treasure, then you will understand the fear of the LORD and find the knowledge of God"* (Proverbs 2:4–5).

Any worthy find requires effort. The Bible is no exception. To understand the Bible, you don't have to be brilliant, but you must be willing to roll up your sleeves and search.

"Do your best to present yourself to God as one approved, a worker who does not need to be ashamed and who correctly handles the word of truth" (2 Timothy 2:15).

Here's a practical point. Study the Bible a bit at a time. Hunger is not satisfied by eating twenty-one meals in one sitting once a week. The body needs a steady diet to remain strong. So does the soul. When God sent food to his people in the wilderness, he didn't provide loaves already made. Instead, he sent them manna in the shape of *"thin flakes like frost on the ground"* (Exodus 16:14).

God gave manna in limited portions.

God sends spiritual food the same way. He opens the heavens with just enough nutrients for today's hunger. He provides *"a rule for this, a rule for that; a little here, a little there"* (Isaiah 28:10).

Don't be discouraged if your reading reaps a small harvest. Some days a lesser portion is all that is needed. What is important is to search every day for that day's message. A steady diet of God's Word over a lifetime builds a healthy soul and mind.

It's much like the little girl who returned from her first day at school feeling a bit dejected. Her mom asked, "Did you learn anything?"

"Apparently not enough," the girl responded. "I have to go back tomorrow, and the next day, and the next . . . "

Such is the case with learning. And such is the case with Bible study. Understanding comes little by little over a lifetime.

There is a third step in understanding the Bible. After the asking and seeking comes the knocking. After you ask and search, *"knock and the door will be opened to you"* (Matthew 7:7).

To knock is to stand at God's door. To make yourself available. To climb the steps, cross the porch, stand at the doorway, and volunteer. Knocking goes beyond the realm of thinking and into the realm of acting.

To knock is to ask, *What can I do? How can I obey? Where can I go?*

It's one thing to know what to do. It's another to do it. But for those who do it—those who choose to obey—a special reward awaits them.

"Whoever looks intently into the perfect law that gives freedom, and continues in it—not forgetting what they have heard, but doing it—they will be blessed in what they do" (James 1:25).

What a promise. Blessings come to those who do what they read in God's Word! It's the same with medicine. If you only read the label but ignore the pills, it won't help. It's the same with food. If you only read the recipe but never cook, you won't be fed. And it's the same with the Bible. If you only read the words but never obey, you'll never know the joy God has promised.

Ask. Search. Knock. Simple, isn't it? So why don't you give it a try? If you do, you'll see why the Bible is the most remarkable book in history.

INTRODUCTION TO
The Gospel of Luke

Nearly 2,000 years ago, a doctor named Luke began a letter to a friend with these words:

> Many have undertaken to draw up an account of the things that have been fulfilled among us, just as they were handed down to us by those who from the first were eyewitnesses and servants of the word. With this in mind, since I myself have carefully investigated everything from the beginning, I too decided to write an orderly account for you, most excellent Theophilus, so that you may know the certainty of the things you have been taught (1:1–4).

Luke and Theophilus shared two loves: a love for Christ and a love for the facts. They didn't want legends; they wanted truth. And so, Dr. Luke began to sort the truth and report the facts to Theophilus. The result is part letter and part research paper.

It is part letter because it was written for a friend. What a bond must have existed between these two that Luke would labor so! It is part research paper because Luke had *studied everything carefully from the beginning,* and he wanted Theophilus to benefit from his study.

Can't you envision Luke in the home of Mary? "Tell me again what happened in Bethlehem." Can't you see him peppering Matthew with questions? "Let me see if I got this parable right." Can't you picture him on long walks with Peter? "When you denied him the third time, did Jesus know?"

With the skill of a surgeon, Luke probes for truth. Why? So his friend could know that what he had been taught was true.

Did Luke have any idea that millions of us would benefit from his study? I doubt it. All he did was share the truth with a friend.

Can you imagine what would happen if we all did the same?

AUTHOR AND DATE

Little is known about Luke, the author of both the Gospel that bears his name and the book of Acts, for he included few personal details about himself in his writings. Early church historians held that he was a native of Antioch in Syria, and there is evidence that he resided in Troas and was a frequent traveling companion of the apostle Paul (see Acts 16:10–17; 20:5–15; 21:1–18; 27:1–28:16). He is first mentioned in Colossians 4:14, where Paul refers to him as a physician, and he is also mentioned in 2 Timothy 4:11 and Philemon 1:24. It is believed that he wrote his Gospel and the book of Acts c. AD 60.

SITUATION

The book of Acts ends with Paul still in Rome, which has led scholars to conclude that Luke wrote his books from Rome during Paul's imprisonment. In his dedication to the "most excellent Theophilus" (Luke 1:3), he indicates he composed his books to provide a carefully ordered account of the events of Jesus' life and birth of the early church. Luke appears to have written his books to a primarily non-Jewish audience, for he frequently stresses Jesus' compassion for those who would have been regarded as outcasts in Jewish society.

KEY THEMES

- Jesus was fully man and fully God.
- Jesus experienced the conflicts of life, yet performed miracles.
- Jesus fulfilled God's mission and taught of God's kingdom.
- Jesus' death and resurrection made possible our relationship with God.

KEY VERSES

You will conceive and give birth to a son, and you are to call him Jesus. He will be great and will be called the Son of the Most High (Luke 1:31–32).

CONTENTS

HOPE IN GOD

"The Lord has done this for me . . . in these days he has shown his favor and taken away my disgrace among the people."

LUKE 1:25

REFLECTION

It's hard not to envy good fortune. Someone else's windfall always raises a few thoughts of *why didn't that happen to me?* Some people can rejoice at others' good fortune, but others become victims of bitterness. Think of a time when God did an amazing work in a friend's life. How did you react? In what ways did that friend's blessing kindle hope in your life?

SITUATION

Having explained to Theophilus the purpose behind his letter, Luke immediately wades into the historical account of Jesus' life. He has to choose a starting point, and he decides the best one is a preliminary event that involves an elderly couple named Zechariah and Elizabeth. Luke's biography of Jesus begins with the birth of John, who became known as the Baptizer.

OBSERVATION

Read Luke 1:5–25 from the New International Version or the New King James Version.

NEW INTERNATIONAL VERSION

5 In the time of Herod king of Judea there was a priest named Zechariah, who belonged to the priestly division of Abijah; his wife Elizabeth was also a descendant of Aaron. 6 Both of them were righteous in the sight of God, observing all the Lord's commands and decrees blamelessly. 7 But they were childless because Elizabeth was not able to conceive, and they were both very old.

⁸ Once when Zechariah's division was on duty and he was serving as priest before God, ⁹ he was chosen by lot, according to the custom of the priesthood, to go into the temple of the Lord and burn incense. ¹⁰ And when the time for the burning of incense came, all the assembled worshipers were praying outside.

¹¹ Then an angel of the Lord appeared to him, standing at the right side of the altar of incense. ¹² When Zechariah saw him, he was startled and was gripped with fear.¹³ But the angel said to him: "Do not be afraid, Zechariah; your prayer has been heard. Your wife Elizabeth will bear you a son, and you are to call him John. ¹⁴ He will be a joy and delight to you, and many will rejoice because of his birth, ¹⁵ for he will be great in the sight of the Lord. He is never to take wine or other fermented drink, and he will be filled with the Holy Spirit even before he is born. ¹⁶ He will bring back many of the people of Israel to the Lord their God. ¹⁷ And he will go on before the Lord, in the spirit and power of Elijah, to turn the hearts of the parents to their children and the disobedient to the wisdom of the righteous—to make ready a people prepared for the Lord."

¹⁸ Zechariah asked the angel, "How can I be sure of this? I am an old man and my wife is well along in years."

¹⁹ The angel said to him, "I am Gabriel. I stand in the presence of God, and I have been sent to speak to you and to tell you this good news. ²⁰ And now you will be silent and not able to speak until the day this happens, because you did not believe my words, which will come true at their appointed time."

²¹ Meanwhile, the people were waiting for Zechariah and wondering why he stayed so long in the temple. ²² When he came out, he could not speak to them. They realized he had seen a vision in the temple, for he kept making signs to them but remained unable to speak.

²³ When his time of service was completed, he returned home. ²⁴ After this his wife Elizabeth became pregnant and for five months remained in seclusion. ²⁵ "The Lord has done this for me," she said. "In these days he has shown his favor and taken away my disgrace among the people."

New King James Version

[5] There was in the days of Herod, the king of Judea, a certain priest named Zacharias, of the division of Abijah. His wife was of the daughters of Aaron, and her name was Elizabeth. [6] And they were both righteous before God, walking in all the commandments and ordinances of the Lord blameless. [7] But they had no child, because Elizabeth was barren, and they were both well advanced in years.

[8] So it was, that while he was serving as priest before God in the order of his division, [9] according to the custom of the priesthood, his lot fell to burn incense when he went into the temple of the Lord. [10] And the whole multitude of the people was praying outside at the hour of incense. [11] Then an angel of the Lord appeared to him, standing on the right side of the altar of incense. [12] And when Zacharias saw him, he was troubled, and fear fell upon him.

[13] But the angel said to him, "Do not be afraid, Zacharias, for your prayer is heard; and your wife Elizabeth will bear you a son, and you shall call his name John. [14] And you will have joy and gladness, and many will rejoice at his birth. [15] For he will be great in the sight of the Lord, and shall drink neither wine nor strong drink. He will also be filled with the Holy Spirit, even from his mother's womb. [16] And he will turn many of the children of Israel to the Lord their God. [17] He will also go before Him in the spirit and power of Elijah, 'to turn the hearts of the fathers to the children,' and the disobedient to the wisdom of the just, to make ready a people prepared for the Lord."

[18] And Zacharias said to the angel, "How shall I know this? For I am an old man, and my wife is well advanced in years."

[19] And the angel answered and said to him, "I am Gabriel, who stands in the presence of God, and was sent to speak to you and bring you these glad tidings. [20] But behold, you will be mute and not able to speak until the day these things take place, because you did not believe my words which will be fulfilled in their own time."

[21] And the people waited for Zacharias, and marveled that he lingered so long in the temple. [22] But when he came out, he could not speak

to them; and they perceived that he had seen a vision in the temple, for he beckoned to them and remained speechless.

[23] So it was, as soon as the days of his service were completed, that he departed to his own house. [24] Now after those days his wife Elizabeth conceived; and she hid herself five months, saying, [25] "Thus the Lord has dealt with me, in the days when He looked on me, to take away my reproach among people."

EXPLORATION

1. What kind of reputation did Zechariah and Elizabeth have in their community?

_____

_____

_____

2. How did Zechariah and Elizabeth cope with the humiliation of childlessness?

_____

_____

_____

3. Where was Zechariah went he met the angel? How did he react to the angel's appearance?

_____

_____

_____

4. The angel promised a child. In what way did this offer hope to Zechariah in his situation?

_____

_____

5. How did Zechariah respond to God's promise? What happened as a result?

_____

_____

_____

6. In what way did Elizabeth react to the fulfillment of the angel's prophecy?

_____

_____

INSPIRATION

We had hoped. How often have you heard a phrase like that?

"We were hoping the doctor would release him."

"I had hoped to pass the exam."

"We had hoped the surgery would get all the tumor."

"I thought the job was in the bag."

Words painted gray with disappointment. What we wanted didn't come. What came, we didn't want. The result? Shattered hope. The foundation of our world trembles. So we trudge up the road . . . dragging our sandals in the dust, wondering what we did to deserve such a plight. "What kind of God would let me down like this?" . . .

Our problem is not so much that God doesn't give us what we hope for as it is that we don't know the right thing for which to hope. (You may want to read that sentence again.)

Hope is not what you expect; it is what you would never dream. It is a wild, improbable tale with a pinch-me-I'm-dreaming ending. It's Abraham adjusting his bifocals so he can see not his grandson, but his son. It's Moses standing in the Promised Land not with Aaron or Miriam at his side, but with Elijah and the transfigured Christ. It's Zechariah left speechless at the sight of his wife Elizabeth, gray-headed and pregnant. And it is the two Emmaus-bound pilgrims reaching out to take a piece of bread only to see the hands from which it is offered are pierced.

Hope is not a granted wish or a favor performed; no, it is far greater than that. It is a zany, unpredictable dependence on a God who loves to surprise us out of our socks and be there in the flesh to see our reaction. (From *God Came Near* by Max Lucado.)

REACTION

7. Why do we, like Zechariah, sometimes doubt God's desire to fulfill our deepest longings?

8. What comfort or encouragement does this passage offer to you when you find yourself in a seemingly hopeless situation?

9. What steps can you take to deal with feelings of hopelessness?

10. In what way does this passage affect your attitude toward your frustrations and problems?

11. What spectacular things are you expecting God to do in your life?

_____

_____

12. In what way can you demonstrate your faith in God's promises?

_____

_____

LIFE LESSONS

There's a difference between expecting God to be faithful and anticipating the specific ways he will demonstrate his faithfulness. The first attitude hopes in God's constancy and wisdom; the second may assume that we know what's best. If we get the two confused, we are liable to be disappointed with the results.

Even though God always gives us good things in the long run, we're sometimes disappointed because he didn't answer our prayers according to our exact agenda. This passage doesn't forbid us to tell God what we want. It simply teaches us to express even our most fervent desires within the boundaries that God ultimately knows best. He sees what we can't see; he knows what we don't know. Sometimes, as in Zechariah and Elizabeth's case, the answer is delayed because a much larger plan is in motion.

DEVOTION

Thank you, Father, for giving us hope in a world of broken promises and dashed dreams. You have proven your trustworthiness by keeping your promises to your people. O Father, you are our only hope. Strengthen our dependence on you, give us patience to wait for your perfect timing, and teach us to rejoice in your goodness.

JOURNALING

What personal hopes or dreams are you tempted to give up on? How can you entrust them to God today?

FOR FURTHER READING

To complete the book of Luke during this twelve-part study, read Luke 1:1–3:38. For more Bible passages on hope, read Psalms 42:5; 62:5; 130:7; Proverbs 23:18; Jeremiah 29:11; Romans 12:12; 15:4; and 1 Timothy 4:9–10; 6:17.

LESSON TWO

FAITH AT WORK

When [Jesus] saw their faith, He said to
him, "Man, your sins are forgiven you."
LUKE 5:20 NKJV

REFLECTION

Faith may be a spiritual concept, but it has practical characteristics that make it an essential component of life. Much of our daily routines are based on what we cannot prove. For instance, we rarely examine a chair before we sit in it . . . or have a car checked out by a mechanic each time we want to drive. We accept many things by faith. But life has a way of testing our faith, particularly when it comes to our relationship with God. Think of a time when you have seen faith at work. What were the results of that faith?

SITUATION

As the crowds grew during the early days of Jesus' ministry, they quickly divided into two camps: the spectators and the participants. On one occasion, Jesus is teaching in a house filled with people clamoring for his attention. Among them are those trying to figure out his plan. Does he fit the "acceptable" categories, or is he a maverick who will soon be forgotten? They are watching his every move and sifting every word. Then the ceiling begins to cave in.

OBSERVATION

*Read Luke 5:17–26 from the New International
Version or the New King James Version.*

New International Version
¹⁷ One day Jesus was teaching, and Pharisees and teachers of the law were sitting there. They had come from every village of Galilee and from Ju-

dea and Jerusalem. And the power of the Lord was with Jesus to heal the sick. [18] Some men came carrying a paralyzed man on a mat and tried to take him into the house to lay him before Jesus. [19] When they could not find a way to do this because of the crowd, they went up on the roof and lowered him on his mat through the tiles into the middle of the crowd, right in front of Jesus.

[20] When Jesus saw their faith, he said, "Friend, your sins are forgiven."

[21] The Pharisees and the teachers of the law began thinking to themselves, "Who is this fellow who speaks blasphemy? Who can forgive sins but God alone?"

[22] Jesus knew what they were thinking and asked, "Why are you thinking these things in your hearts? [23] Which is easier: to say, 'Your sins are forgiven,' or to say, 'Get up and walk'? [24] But I want you to know that the Son of Man has authority on earth to forgive sins." So he said to the paralyzed man, "I tell you, get up, take your mat and go home." [25] Immediately he stood up in front of them, took what he had been lying on and went home praising God. [26] Everyone was amazed and gave praise to God. They were filled with awe and said, "We have seen remarkable things today."

New King James Version

[17] Now it happened on a certain day, as He was teaching, that there were Pharisees and teachers of the law sitting by, who had come out of every town of Galilee, Judea, and Jerusalem. And the power of the Lord was present to heal them. [18] Then behold, men brought on a bed a man who was paralyzed, whom they sought to bring in and lay before Him. [19] And when they could not find how they might bring him in, because of the crowd, they went up on the housetop and let him down with his bed through the tiling into the midst before Jesus.

[20] When He saw their faith, He said to him, "Man, your sins are forgiven you."

[21] And the scribes and the Pharisees began to reason, saying, "Who is this who speaks blasphemies? Who can forgive sins but God alone?"

[22] But when Jesus perceived their thoughts, He answered and said to them, "Why are you reasoning in your hearts? [23] Which is easier, to say, 'Your sins are forgiven you,' or to say, 'Rise up and walk'? [24] But that you may know that the Son of Man has power on earth to forgive sins"—He said to the man who was paralyzed, "I say to you, arise, take up your bed, and go to your house."

[25] Immediately he rose up before them, took up what he had been lying on, and departed to his own house, glorifying God. [26] And they were all amazed, and they glorified God and were filled with fear, saying, "We have seen strange things today!"

EXPLORATION

1. As this scene opens, who are present among the crowd? Why do you think they had traveled there from faraway places to see Jesus?

_____

_____

_____

2. A group of men in the crowd that day had decided to bring their paralyzed friend to Jesus. What do you think they hoped Jesus would do for him?

_____

_____

_____

3. What risks and obstacles did the men face because of the crowd around Christ?

_____

_____

4. What were the pros and cons of their plan to let their friend down through the roof?

_____

_____

_____

5. What did these men's actions—and the fact they would go to any length to get their friend to Jesus—reveal about their perception of Christ?

_____

_____

_____

6. Why was Jesus' first response to forgive rather than to heal?

_____

_____

_____

INSPIRATION

Let's talk for a minute about lovebursts. . . . Spontaneous affection. Tender moments of radiant love. Ignited devotion. Explosions of tenderness. . . .

They remind you about what matters. A telegram delivered to the back door of the familiar, telling you to treasure the treasure you've got while you've got it. A whisper from an angel, or someone who sounds like one, reminding you that what you have is greater than what you want and that what is urgent is not always what matters.

Those are lovebursts. You have them. I have them. And this may surprise you: Jesus had them . . . lots of them. One of them happened when Jesus met an invalid. The man couldn't walk. He couldn't stand. His limbs were bent and his body twisted. . . .

[The man's] friends want him to heal their friend. But Jesus won't settle for a simple healing of the body—he wants to heal the soul. He leapfrogs the physical and deals with the spiritual. To heal the body is temporal; to heal the soul is eternal.

The request of the friends is valid—but timid. The expectations of the crowd are high—but not high enough. They expect Jesus to say, "I heal you." Instead he says, "I forgive you."

They expect him to treat the body, for that is what they see.

He chooses to treat not only the body, but also the spiritual, for that is what he sees.

They want Jesus to give the man a new body so he can walk. Jesus gives grace so the man can live.

Remarkable. Sometimes God is so touched by what he sees that he gives us what we need and not simply that for which we ask.

It's a good thing. For who would have ever thought to ask God for what he gives? Which of us would have dared to say: "God, would you please hang yourself on a tool of torture as a substitution for every mistake I have ever committed?" And then have the audacity to add: "And after you forgive me, could you prepare me a place in your house to live forever?"

And if that wasn't enough: "And would you please live within me and protect me and guide me and bless me with more than I could ever deserve?"

Honestly, would we have the chutzpah to ask for that? No, we, like the friends, would have only asked for the small stuff.

We would ask for little things like a long life and a healthy body and a good job. Grand requests from our perspective, but from God's it's like taking the moped when he offers the limo. (From He Still Moves Stones by Max Lucado.)

REACTION

7. In what way did the four friends' faith in Jesus affect the life of the paralyzed man?

_____

_____

_____

8. In what ways does your faith affect others around you?

9. What are some ways that you can show your faith in Jesus Christ?

10. What risks or obstacles have you faced in living out your beliefs?

11. How have those difficulties stretched and strengthened your faith?

12. In what ways have you seen God bless people who trust him?

LIFE LESSONS

This episode in Jesus' life offers us two challenging examples as we seek to live as disciples of Jesus. We can identify with the paralyzed man, and we can identify with his friends. Each role requires a certain kind of faith. The paralyzed man trusted both his friends and Jesus. We don't know if he asked them for help or if he just went along with their plan, but feeling himself lowered through the roof must have been a moment of testing.

The friends had to escalate their faith to meet the obstacles they encountered, and their persistence was rewarded. We can experience the same kinds of rewards for exercising our faith in God throughout life. The paralyzed man was not only healed but also forgiven. This reminds us that no matter how bold our faith, God's capacity to go beyond what we could ask or imagine will not be exceeded.

DEVOTION

Father, when all the doors are closed, give us the courage to persevere. When no solutions are in sight, help us to find new ways to break through the barriers that separate us from you. May we persistently seek your face and daily demonstrate our faith in you.

JOURNALING

What bold step of faith are you willing to take this week to be closer to God?

_____

_____

_____

_____

_____

_____

FOR FURTHER READING

To complete the book of Luke during this twelve-part study, read Luke 4:1–5:39. For more Bible passages on faith, read Romans 4:16–25; 1 Corinthians 16:13; 2 Corinthians 5:7; Galatians 2:16; Philippians 3:8–9; 1 Timothy 6:11–12; Hebrews 11:1–2; James 2:14–26.

LESSON THREE

A NEW STANDARD

Jesus said to them, "I ask you, which is lawful on the Sabbath:
to do good or to do evil, to save life or to destroy it?"
LUKE 6:9

REFLECTION

All of us at times feel the pressure of not measuring up to the standards we set for ourselves. When is a time in your life that you set an expectation for yourself that you couldn't meet? What did you learn through the experience about forgiving yourself and accepting God's grace?

SITUATION

Curfews come in many shapes and sizes. Jesus lived in a land of Sabbath curfew. The third of the Ten Commandments, "Remember the Sabbath day by keeping it holy" (Exodus 20:8), had been scrutinized and applied so closely that the spirit and purpose of God's gift of Sabbath had been lost. The controversy Jesus stirred up by honoring God on the Sabbath seems almost irrational to us, yet it shows that legalism without heart often produces harsh results. Jesus was chastised by the religious leaders for doing something on the Sabbath that they couldn't do even on their best day. They devalued the healing he offered on the Sabbath because they were more concerned with keeping up appearances than with pleasing God.

OBSERVATION

Read Luke 6:1–11 from the New International Version or the New King James Version.

New International Version
¹ One Sabbath Jesus was going through the grainfields, and his disciples began to pick some heads of grain, rub them in their hands and eat the

kernels. [2] Some of the Pharisees asked, "Why are you doing what is unlawful on the Sabbath?"

[3] Jesus answered them, "Have you never read what David did when he and his companions were hungry? [4] He entered the house of God, and taking the consecrated bread, he ate what is lawful only for priests to eat. And he also gave some to his companions." [5] Then Jesus said to them, "The Son of Man is Lord of the Sabbath."

[6] On another Sabbath he went into the synagogue and was teaching, and a man was there whose right hand was shriveled. [7] The Pharisees and the teachers of the law were looking for a reason to accuse Jesus, so they watched him closely to see if he would heal on the Sabbath. [8] But Jesus knew what they were thinking and said to the man with the shriveled hand, "Get up and stand in front of everyone." So he got up and stood there.

[9] Then Jesus said to them, "I ask you, which is lawful on the Sabbath: to do good or to do evil, to save life or to destroy it?"

[10] He looked around at them all, and then said to the man, "Stretch out your hand." He did so, and his hand was completely restored. [11] But the Pharisees and the teachers of the law were furious and began to discuss with one another what they might do to Jesus.

New King James Version

[1] Now it happened on the second Sabbath after the first that He went through the grainfields. And His disciples plucked the heads of grain and ate them, rubbing them in their hands. [2] And some of the Pharisees said to them, "Why are you doing what is not lawful to do on the Sabbath?"

[3] But Jesus answering them said, "Have you not even read this, what David did when he was hungry, he and those who were with him: [4] how he went into the house of God, took and ate the showbread, and also gave some to those with him, which is not lawful for any but the priests to eat?" [5] And He said to them, "The Son of Man is also Lord of the Sabbath."

[6] Now it happened on another Sabbath, also, that He entered the synagogue and taught. And a man was there whose right hand was

withered. ⁷ So the scribes and Pharisees watched Him closely, whether He would heal on the Sabbath, that they might find an accusation against Him. ⁸ But He knew their thoughts, and said to the man who had the withered hand, "Arise and stand here." And he arose and stood. ⁹ Then Jesus said to them, "I will ask you one thing: Is it lawful on the Sabbath to do good or to do evil, to save life or to destroy?" ¹⁰ And when He had looked around at them all, He said to the man, "Stretch out your hand." And he did so, and his hand was restored as whole as the other. ¹¹ But they were filled with rage, and discussed with one another what they might do to Jesus.

EXPLORATION

1. What did the disciples do at the beginning of this passage that provided the grounds for the Pharisees to question Jesus?

_____

_____

_____

_____

2. How did Jesus deal with these accusations? How did he use the story of David and his men (see 1 Samuel 21:1–9) to refute the religious leaders' claim?

_____

_____

_____

_____

3. What was Jesus stating about himself when he said he was Lord of the Sabbath? How would the religious leaders have interpreted this?

_____

_____

_____

_____

4. Why do you think the Pharisees and teachers of the law were so intent on "looking for a reason to accuse Jesus" (verse 7)?

_____

_____

_____

5. How did Jesus respond to religious leaders' scrutiny when it came to healing the man with the shriveled hand?

_____

_____

_____

6. What do these stories tell you about the way in which God wants us to love others?

_____

_____

INSPIRATION

Suppose you, for most of your life, have had a heart condition. Your frail pumper restricts your activities. Each morning at work when the healthy employees take the stairs, you wait for the elevator.

But then comes the transplant. A healthy heart is placed within you. After recovery, you return to work and encounter the flight of stairs— the same flight of stairs you earlier avoided. By habit, you start for the elevator. But then you remember. You aren't the same person. You have a new heart. Within you dwells a new power.

Do you live like the old person or the new? Do you count yourself as having a new heart or old? You have a choice to make. You might say, "I can't climb stairs; I'm too weak." Does your choice negate the presence of a new heart? Dismiss the work of the surgeon? No. Choosing the elevator would suggest only one fact—you haven't learned to trust your new power.

It takes time. But at some point you've got to try those stairs. You've got to test the new ticker. You've got to experiment with the new you. For if you don't, you will run out of steam.

Religious rule keeping can sap your strength. It's endless. There is always another class to attend . . . another Sabbath to obey. No prison is as endless as the prison of perfection. Her inmates find work but never find peace. How could they? They never know when they are finished.

Christ, however, gifts you with a finished work. He fulfilled the law for you. Bid farewell to the burden of religion. Gone is the fear that having done everything, you might not have done enough. You climb the stairs, not by your strength, but his. God pledges to help those who stop trying to help themselves.

"He who began a good work in you will carry it on to completion until the day of Christ Jesus" (Philippians 1:6). God will change you from the inside out. When he is finished, he'll even let you sit at his table. (From *Next Door Savior* by Max Lucado.)

REACTION

7. What lessons can you learn from Jesus' example about religious rule keeping?

_____

_____

_____

_____

8. What is the real issue at stake when it comes to trying to live up to the letter of the law? How is the quest for perfection like being in an endless prison?

_____

_____

_____

_____

9. What happens when we try to do God's work in our own strength?

_____

_____

_____

10. In what way does Jesus' response to the religious leaders inspire you to change the way you deal with your job or ministry?

_____

_____

_____

11. How are you tapping into the power of Jesus today? What do you need to do to let go of perfectionism and live in the freedom that Jesus provides?

_____

_____

_____

12. What practical steps can you take to depend more on God to help you face the challenges in your daily life?

_____

_____

_____

LIFE LESSONS

The balance in Jesus' life between time spent with God in prayer and time spent in Scripture explains many of his responses. He based answers on God's Word, demonstrating that he had spent time thinking through ways in which the Scriptures could be used, as well as misused. The religious leaders misused Scripture. When they were only concerned about the law and keeping the Sabbath, the real purpose for the Sabbath was neglected and lost. Jesus challenges us to ask the questions, "Do I know why I'm obeying? Am I doing this for the right reasons?"

DEVOTION

Lord, help us to follow in your footsteps and always be willing to serve those in need. Help us to live in the freedom that you have given us rather than our own concepts of godliness. When we face difficult decisions, enable us to turn to you for guidance. And when life is easy, keep us from thinking that we can make it on our own. Remind us that only you can help us live victoriously.

JOURNALING

What is an area in your life in which you need to rely more on God's strength than your own?

_____

_____

_____

_____

_____

_____

_____

_____

_____

_____

FOR FURTHER READING

To complete the book of Luke during this twelve-part study, read Luke 6:1–49. For more Bible passages on the benefits of prayer, read Deuteronomy 4:7; 2 Chronicles 7:14; Matthew 21:22; Mark 11:22–26; Philippians 4:6–7; 1 Timothy 4:4–5; James 5:13–18.

LESSON FOUR

CHRIST'S COMPASSION

When the Lord saw her, He had compassion
on her and said to her, "Do not weep."
LUKE 7:13 NKJV

REFLECTION

Compassion frequently arrives in little gestures, such as a tactful suggestion for someone to watch his or her step to avoid injury. Compassion also makes larger gestures, such as pulling out of traffic to change a tire for a stranded motorist on the side of the road. Think of a time when someone showed compassion to you. How did it make you feel?

SITUATION

As Jesus' popularity grew, it became increasingly complicated for him to travel. A crowd followed him everywhere he went. When he approached the village of Nain one day, the effect of the people might have been called a "crush hour"—and all the more because a procession of villagers was leaving town for a funeral. The two crowds met on the edge of town.

OBSERVATION

Read Luke 7:11–23 from the New International
Version or the New King James Version.

NEW INTERNATIONAL VERSION

[11] Soon afterward, Jesus went to a town called Nain, and his disciples and a large crowd went along with him. [12] As he approached the town gate, a dead person was being carried out—the only son of his mother, and she was a widow. And a large crowd from the town was with her. [13] When the Lord saw her, his heart went out to her and he said, "Don't cry."

[14] Then he went up and touched the bier they were carrying him on, and the bearers stood still. He said, "Young man, I say to you, get up!" [15] The dead man sat up and began to talk, and Jesus gave him back to his mother.

[16] They were all filled with awe and praised God. "A great prophet has appeared among us," they said. "God has come to help his people." [17] This news about Jesus spread throughout Judea and the surrounding country.

[18] John's disciples told him about all these things. Calling two of them, [19] he sent them to the Lord to ask, "Are you the one who is to come, or should we expect someone else?"

[20] When the men came to Jesus, they said, "John the Baptist sent us to you to ask, 'Are you the one who is to come, or should we expect someone else?'"

[21] At that very time Jesus cured many who had diseases, sicknesses and evil spirits, and gave sight to many who were blind. [22] So he replied to the messengers, "Go back and report to John what you have seen and heard: The blind receive sight, the lame walk, those who have leprosy are cleansed, the deaf hear, the dead are raised, and the good news is proclaimed to the poor. [23] Blessed is anyone who does not stumble on account of me."

NEW KING JAMES VERSION

[11] Now it happened, the day after, that He went into a city called Nain; and many of His disciples went with Him, and a large crowd. [12] And when He came near the gate of the city, behold, a dead man was being carried out, the only son of his mother; and she was a widow. And a large crowd from the city was with her. [13] When the Lord saw her, He had compassion on her and said to her, "Do not weep." [14] Then He came and touched the open coffin, and those who carried him stood still. And He said, "Young man, I say to you, arise." [15] So he who was dead sat up and began to speak. And He presented him to his mother.

[16] Then fear came upon all, and they glorified God, saying, "A great prophet has risen up among us"; and, "God has visited His people." [17] And this report about Him went throughout all Judea and all the surrounding region.

¹⁸ Then the disciples of John reported to him concerning all these things. ¹⁹ And John, calling two of his disciples to him, sent them to Jesus, saying, "Are You the Coming One, or do we look for another?"

²⁰ When the men had come to Him, they said, "John the Baptist has sent us to You, saying, 'Are You the Coming One, or do we look for another?'" ²¹ And that very hour He cured many of infirmities, afflictions, and evil spirits; and to many blind He gave sight.

²² Jesus answered and said to them, "Go and tell John the things you have seen and heard: that the blind see, the lame walk, the lepers are cleansed, the deaf hear, the dead are raised, the poor have the gospel preached to them. ²³ And blessed is he who is not offended because of Me."

EXPLORATION

1. Jesus and his followers encountered a funeral procession near the city of Nain. Why do you think Jesus chose to raise the boy back to life?

_____

_____

_____

2. How did Jesus show compassion for the people in the funeral procession?

_____

_____

_____

_____

3. How did Jesus specifically show his compassion for the mother who had lost her son?

_____

_____

_____

_____

4. What good came from the miracle Jesus performed?

_____

_____

_____

_____

5. What do you think prompted John the Baptist to send two messengers to Christ?

_____

_____

_____

_____

6. What does it mean to stumble or be offended in your faith?

_____

_____

_____

_____

INSPIRATION

Two crowds. One entering the city and one leaving. They couldn't be more diverse. The group arriving buzzes with laughter and conversation. They follow Jesus. The group leaving the city is solemn—a herd of sadness hypnotized by the requiem of death. Above them rides the reason for their grief—a cold body on a wicker stretcher.

The woman at the back of the procession is the mother. She has walked this trail before. It seems like just yesterday she buried the body of her husband. Her son walked with her then. Now she walks alone, quarantined in her sadness. . . .

The followers of Jesus stop and step aside as the procession shadows by. The blanket of mourning muffles the laughter of the disciples. No one spoke. What could they say? . . .

Jesus, however, knew what to say and what to do. When he saw the mother, his heart began to break . . . and his lips began to tighten. He glared at the angel of death that hovered over the body of the boy. "Not this time, Satan. This boy is mine."

At that moment the mother walked in front of him. Jesus spoke to her. "Don't cry." She stopped and looked into this stranger's face. If she wasn't shocked by his presumption, you can bet some of the witnesses were.

Don't cry? *Don't cry?* What kind of request is that? A request only God can make.

Jesus stepped toward the bier and touched it. The pallbearers stopped marching. The mourners ceased moaning. As Jesus stared at the boy, the crowd was silent. Jesus turned his attention to the dead boy. "Young man," his voice was calm, "come back to life again."

The living stood motionless as the dead came to life. Wooden fingers moved. Gray-pale cheeks blushed. The dead man sat up. . . .

Jesus must have smiled as the two embraced. Stunned, the crowd broke into cheers and applause. They hugged each other and slapped Jesus on the back. Someone proclaimed the undeniable, "God has come to help his people."

Jesus gave the woman much more than her son. He gave her a secret—a whisper that was overheard by us. "That," he said pointing at the cot, "that is fantasy. This," he grinned, putting an arm around the boy, "this is reality." (From *Six Hours One Friday* by Max Lucado.)

REACTION

7. What do you think motivated Jesus to heal the sick, deliver the demon-possessed, and give sight to the blind?

_____

_____

_____

_____

8. What new insight can you gain about Jesus' character from this passage?

_____

_____

_____

9. What difference does it make in our lives to know that Jesus had mercy on people?

_____

_____

_____

10. What tends to keep you from acknowledging and appreciating what Jesus has done for you?

_____

_____

_____

11. In what tangible way can you thank Jesus for the love and mercy he has shown to you?

_____

_____

_____

12. Think of one person to whom you could show more Christian compassion. What has kept you from taking action on that awareness?

_____

_____

_____

LIFE LESSONS

Compassion grows out of our faith and obedience. We don't practice compassion just because it "works." We treat others with compassion because Jesus showed compassion and we want to emulate him, and because all people are loved by God. One way to look at it is this: treat people in such a way that if they want to take revenge on you, they will have to be nice. If you want to take seriously Jesus' call to discipleship, you have to honestly consider if you have treated those whom God has placed into your life today with compassion.

DEVOTION

Lord, thank you for taking the time to keep a poor widow from a life of loneliness. Thank you for the length you went to in order to express care. It helps us see your power over death and your deep love and compassion for needy people. Our hearts overflow with gratitude for the mercy you have shown to us. Receive our praise and help us to show your love to the people around us.

JOURNALING

How has Jesus shown compassion to you? How are you demonstrating compassion to others?

_____

_____

_____

_____

_____

_____

FOR FURTHER READING

To complete the book of Luke during this twelve-part study, read Luke 7:1–50. For more Bible passages on Christ's compassion, read Matthew 9:35–36; 14:13–14; 15:32–39; 20:29–34; and Mark 1:40–42; 6:34; 8:2.

CHRIST'S AUTHORITY

A large herd of pigs was feeding there on the hillside. The demons begged Jesus to let them go into the pigs, and he gave them permission.

LUKE 8:32

REFLECTION

Members of a society live under the authority of those in power, whether that is a boss, a police officer, a government official, or even a parent. How do you typically respond to those who are in authority over you? How do act toward those over whom you have authority?

_____

_____

_____

_____

SITUATION

During his time on earth, Jesus showed compassion those who were suffering and brought healing into their lives. Many times this took the form of physical healings, in which Jesus restored a blind person's sight, or made a paralyzed person walk again, or even raised someone from the dead. But at other times, the healing took the form of freeing a person from the stronghold of the enemy. In one such encounter in the region of the Gerasenes, Jesus displayed his ultimate authority over the forces of darkness by freeing a man from demons.

OBSERVATION

Read Luke 8:26–39 from the New International
Version or the New King James Version.

New International Version

²⁶ They sailed to the region of the Gerasenes, which is across the lake from Galilee. ²⁷ When Jesus stepped ashore, he was met by a demon-possessed man from the town. For a long time this man had not worn clothes or lived in a house, but had lived in the tombs. ²⁸ When he saw

Jesus, he cried out and fell at his feet, shouting at the top of his voice, "What do you want with me, Jesus, Son of the Most High God? I beg you, don't torture me!" [29] For Jesus had commanded the impure spirit to come out of the man. Many times it had seized him, and though he was chained hand and foot and kept under guard, he had broken his chains and had been driven by the demon into solitary places.

[30] Jesus asked him, "What is your name?"

"Legion," he replied, because many demons had gone into him. [31] And they begged Jesus repeatedly not to order them to go into the Abyss.

[32] A large herd of pigs was feeding there on the hillside. The demons begged Jesus to let them go into the pigs, and he gave them permission. [33] When the demons came out of the man, they went into the pigs, and the herd rushed down the steep bank into the lake and was drowned.

[34] When those tending the pigs saw what had happened, they ran off and reported this in the town and countryside, [35] and the people went out to see what had happened. When they came to Jesus, they found the man from whom the demons had gone out, sitting at Jesus' feet, dressed and in his right mind; and they were afraid. [36] Those who had seen it told the people how the demon-possessed man had been cured. [37] Then all the people of the region of the Gerasenes asked Jesus to leave them, because they were overcome with fear. So he got into the boat and left.

[38] The man from whom the demons had gone out begged to go with him, but Jesus sent him away, saying, [39] "Return home and tell how much God has done for you." So the man went away and told all over town how much Jesus had done for him.

NEW KING JAMES VERSION

[26] Then they sailed to the country of the Gadarenes, which is opposite Galilee. [27] And when He stepped out on the land, there met Him a certain man from the city who had demons for a long time. And he wore no clothes, nor did he live in a house but in the tombs. [28] When he saw Jesus, he cried out, fell down before Him, and with a loud voice said, "What have I to do with You, Jesus, Son of the Most High God? I beg

You, do not torment me!" ²⁹ For He had commanded the unclean spirit to come out of the man. For it had often seized him, and he was kept under guard, bound with chains and shackles; and he broke the bonds and was driven by the demon into the wilderness.

³⁰ Jesus asked him, saying, "What is your name?"

And he said, "Legion," because many demons had entered him. ³¹ And they begged Him that He would not command them to go out into the abyss.

³² Now a herd of many swine was feeding there on the mountain. So they begged Him that He would permit them to enter them. And He permitted them. ³³ Then the demons went out of the man and entered the swine, and the herd ran violently down the steep place into the lake and drowned.

³⁴ When those who fed them saw what had happened, they fled and told it in the city and in the country. ³⁵ Then they went out to see what had happened, and came to Jesus, and found the man from whom the demons had departed, sitting at the feet of Jesus, clothed and in his right mind. And they were afraid. ³⁶ They also who had seen it told them by what means he who had been demon-possessed was healed. ³⁷ Then the whole multitude of the surrounding region of the Gadarenes asked Him to depart from them, for they were seized with great fear. And He got into the boat and returned.

³⁸ Now the man from whom the demons had departed begged Him that he might be with Him. But Jesus sent him away, saying, ³⁹ "Return to your own house, and tell what great things God has done for you." And he went his way and proclaimed throughout the whole city what great things Jesus had done for him.

EXPLORATION

1. What was the situation in which the demon-possessed man was living?

_____

_____

_____

_____

2. What did the demons in the man say to Jesus? How did Jesus respond?

3. How did Jesus demonstrate his authority over the demons?

4. How did the people in the town react to the news that the man had been delivered?

5. How did the man who had been delivered respond to Jesus?

6. What does this story say about those whom society has deemed "too far gone" to save?

INSPIRATION

Where did Jesus go to find his first missionary? (*You won't believe this.*) A cemetery. Who was the first ambassador he commissioned? (*You're not going to buy this either.*) A lunatic. The man Jesus sent out was a madman turned missionary. . . .

He's the man your mom told you to avoid. He's the fellow the police routinely lock up. He's the deranged man who stalks neighborhoods and murders families. This is the face that fills the screen during the evening news.

And this is the first missionary of the church.

Palestine didn't know what to do with him. They restrained him, but he broke the chains. He ripped off his clothes. He lived in caves. He cut himself with rocks. He was a rabid coyote on the loose, a menace to society. Of absolutely no good to anyone. No one had a place for him—except Jesus.

Even today the best that modern medicine could offer such a man is medication and extensive treatment. Maybe, with much time, expense, and professional help, such destructive behavior could be curtailed. But it would take years.

With Jesus, it takes seconds.

The encounter is explosive. The disciples' boat beaches near a grave-yard and a herd of pigs. Both are ritually and culturally unclean for Jews. As Jesus steps out, a crazy man storms out of a cavern. Wild hair. Bloody wrists. Scratched skin. Fury encased in flesh. Naked bedlam. Arms flailing and voice screaming. The apostles gawk and gulp and put a foot back in the boat.

They are horrified. But Jesus isn't. . . .

Jesus wants the man back. The demons muster no challenge. They offer no threat. They've heard this voice before. When God demands, the demons have one response. They plead.

"They begged Jesus repeatedly not to order them to go into the Abyss" (Luke 8:31). Jesus' mere appearance humbles the demons. Though they had dominated this man, they cower before God. Though they had laced a region with fear, they beg for mercy from Jesus. His words reduce them to sniveling, groveling weaklings.

Feeling safer in a herd of pigs than in the presence of God, the demons ask to be sent into the swine. Jesus consents, and 2,000 possessed pigs hurl themselves into the sea.

And all the while the disciples do nothing. While Jesus fights, the followers stare. They don't know anything else to do.

Can you relate? Are you watching a world out of control and don't know what to do? If so, do what the disciples did: when the fighting is fierce, stand back and let the Father fight. (From *He Still Moves Stones* by Max Lucado.)

REACTION

7. What does this story reveal about the people God uses for his service?

_____

_____

_____

_____

8. How does this story give you hope that Jesus can deliver you from anything you face?

_____

_____

_____

_____

9. How does this story compel you to show compassion for the outcasts of society?

_____

_____

_____

_____

10. While Jesus fought the enemy, his followers watched in awe. What are some battles that you need Jesus to take on for you today?

_____

_____

_____

_____

11. What are some practical steps you will take to trust in Christ and go to him in prayer when you feel under attack?

_____

_____

_____

12. Who are some people in your life who need to experience the power of Christ? What will be your prayer for them today?

_____

_____

_____

LIFE LESSONS

The story of the man living in the tombs of the Gerasenes offers us a sobering reality: we live in a world in which the forces of evil are present and at work. We have a real enemy named Satan, and he seeks to bring destruction and ruin to our lives. Yet equally evident from the story is that Jesus has the authority over the darkness in our world. It's not even close—when Jesus commands, the demons have no other options but to plead and obey. We serve a God who is not only compassionate and loving toward us but in ultimate control over everything. We need to remember to lean on his strength when we are in a situation out of our control.

DEVOTION

Thank you, Father, not only for the compassion you show to us but also for the authority you give us in your name. Help us today to remember that you are the Source of our life and to lean into you when situations come our way that we cannot overcome. Thank you for fighting on our behalf.

JOURNALING

What is situation in your life that feels out of control? What deliverance do you need from God?

FOR FURTHER READING

To complete the book of Luke during this twelve-part study, read Luke 8:1–56. For more Bible passages on obeying the Bible, read Leviticus 18:4–5; Deuteronomy 13:4; Joshua 22:5; John 14:23; Romans 2:13; 1 John 3:24; 2 John 1:6; Revelation 14:12.

LESSON SIX

BELIEVING IN JESUS

"Whoever wants to be my disciple must deny themselves and take up their cross daily and follow me. For whoever wants to save their life will lose it, but whoever loses their life for me will save it."

LUKE 9:23–24

45

REFLECTION

There are many opinions about who Jesus is, but a consensus is hard to find. Maybe the differences in conclusions about Jesus' identity are more a reflection of the people who are commenting. How would your friends and coworkers answer the question, "Who is Jesus?"

SITUATION

After delivering the man in the Gerasenes from demons, Jesus called his twelve disciples together and gave them the power and authority to do the same. He told them to travel from village to village, proclaiming the kingdom of God and healing the sick. Later, the disciples returned to report on their efforts, and Jesus took them aside for a rest. That break didn't last long, as the crowds who followed interrupted them. This led to the feeding of more than 5,000 people in the wilderness. Shortly after these events, Jesus' own quiet time of prayer led up to asking his disciples a disquieting question: *What were people saying about him?*

OBSERVATION

Read Luke 9:18–27 from the New International
Version or the New King James Version.

New International Version
¹⁸ Once when Jesus was praying in private and his disciples were with him, he asked them, "Who do the crowds say I am?"

[19] They replied, "Some say John the Baptist; others say Elijah; and still others, that one of the prophets of long ago has come back to life."

[20] "But what about you?" he asked. "Who do you say I am?"

Peter answered, "God's Messiah."

[21] Jesus strictly warned them not to tell this to anyone. [22] And he said, "The Son of Man must suffer many things and be rejected by the elders, the chief priests and the teachers of the law, and he must be killed and on the third day be raised to life."

[23] Then he said to them all: "Whoever wants to be my disciple must deny themselves and take up their cross daily and follow me. [24] For whoever wants to save their life will lose it, but whoever loses their life for me will save it. [25] What good is it for someone to gain the whole world, and yet lose or forfeit their very self? [26] Whoever is ashamed of me and my words, the Son of Man will be ashamed of them when he comes in his glory and in the glory of the Father and of the holy angels.

[27] "Truly I tell you, some who are standing here will not taste death before they see the kingdom of God."

NEW KING JAMES VERSION

[18] And it happened, as He was alone praying, that His disciples joined Him, and He asked them, saying, "Who do the crowds say that I am?"

[19] So they answered and said, "John the Baptist, but some say Elijah; and others say that one of the old prophets has risen again."

[20] He said to them, "But who do you say that I am?"

Peter answered and said, "The Christ of God."

[21] And He strictly warned and commanded them to tell this to no one, [22] saying, "The Son of Man must suffer many things, and be rejected by the elders and chief priests and scribes, and be killed, and be raised the third day."

[23] Then He said to them all, "If anyone desires to come after Me, let him deny himself, and take up his cross daily, and follow Me. [24] For whoever desires to save his life will lose it, but whoever loses his life for My sake will save it. [25] For what profit is it to a man if he gains the whole world, and is

himself destroyed or lost? [26] For whoever is ashamed of Me and My words, of him the Son of Man will be ashamed when He comes in His own glory, and in His Father's, and of the holy angels. [27] But I tell you truly, there are some standing here who shall not taste death till they see the kingdom of God."

EXPLORATION

1. Why do you think Jesus posed probing questions to his disciples about his identity?

_____

_____

_____

_____

2. What different views did people have about Jesus' identity? What was Peter's view?

_____

_____

_____

_____

3. Why do you think Jesus warned the disciples to keep his true identity a secret?

_____

_____

_____

_____

4. What does it mean to "take up your cross" daily? How is this done?

_____

_____

_____

_____

5. What kind of commitment is required to follow Jesus?

_____

_____

_____

_____

_____

6. What are some of the rewards of sacrificing your life to follow Jesus?

_____

_____

_____

_____

INSPIRATION

One of the most dramatic scenes in the New Testament occurred in a city known as Caesarea Philippi. In the midst of this carnival of marble columns and golden idols, a penniless, homeless, nameless Nazarene asks his band of followers, "Who do you say that I am?"

The immensity of the question is staggering. I would imagine that Peter's answer did not come without some hesitation. Shuffling of feet. Anxious silence. How absurd that this man should be the Son of God. No trumpets. No purple robes. No armies. Yet there was that glint of determination in his eye and that edge of certainty in his message. Peter's response sliced the silence. "I believe that you are . . . the Son of God."

Many have looked at Jesus; but few have seen him. Many have seen his shadow, his people, his story. But only a handful have seen Jesus. Only a few have looked through the fog of religiosity and found him. Only a few have dared to stand eye-to-eye and heart to heart with Jesus and say, "I believe that you are the Son of God." (From _Shaped by God_ by Max Lucado.)

REACTION

7. Why is Jesus' identity crucial to your faith?

_____

_____

_____

8. What are some answers people give today about the identify of Jesus?

_____

_____

_____

9. How would you explain what you believe about Jesus to a person who has never heard his name?

_____

_____

_____

10. What opportunities have you had to proclaim your faith in Jesus?

_____

_____

_____

11. In what circumstances is it difficult for you to share your views about Christ?

_____

_____

_____

12. In what way does this passage motivate you to speak out about your faith in Jesus?

_____

_____

_____

_____

LIFE LESSONS

In today's world, there is no shortage of ideas and opinions about Jesus. Ultimately, what matters in our relationship with Christ is what *we* say about him. Saying nothing about him may be an option we take, but not one that expresses the kind of witness and honor Jesus deserves from those who claim to be his followers.

DEVOTION

Lord Jesus, we believe that you are the Son of God. We want to follow you, but sometimes we are scared of the risks and costs involved. But your Word teaches us that any sacrifice we make will be well worth the eternal reward. So we ask you to take our focus off of the things of this world and set our hopes on spending eternity with you.

JOURNALING

What things do you need to give up in your life to follow Jesus wholeheartedly?

_____

_____

_____

_____

_____

FOR FURTHER READING

To complete the book of Luke during this twelve-part study, read Luke 9:1–10:42. For more Bible passages on believing in Jesus, read John 3:14–18; 13:19–20; 20:24–31; Acts 16:31; Romans 3:22; Philippians 1:29; 1 Thessalonians 4:14; and 1 John 5:1–12.

PERSISTENT PRAYER

*"So I say to you, ask, and it will be given to you; seek,
and you will find; knock, and it will be opened to you.
For everyone who asks receives, and he who seeks
finds, and to him who knocks it will be opened."*

LUKE 11:9–10 NKJV

REFLECTION

Think of a time when you felt like giving up on a certain prayer request. What made it difficult to pray? What helped you keep on praying? What do you think would have happened if you stopped praying?

_____

_____

_____

_____

SITUATION

The disciples had numerous opportunities to observe Jesus as he prayed. Eventually, they got around to saying, "Lord, teach us to pray." Jesus' response shows that he heard two requests in one: the disciples needed some idea of *how* to pray and they also needed some idea of *why* they should pray. He gave them a model for how to approach God, and he also gave reasons why they should pray.

OBSERVATION

Read Luke 11:1–13 from the New International Version or the New King James Version.

New International Version

¹ One day Jesus was praying in a certain place. When he finished, one of his disciples said to him, "Lord, teach us to pray, just as John taught his disciples."

² He said to them, "When you pray, say:

"'Father,
hallowed be your name,

your kingdom come.

³ Give us each day our daily bread.

⁴ Forgive us our sins,

for we also forgive everyone who sins against us.

And lead us not into temptation.'"

⁵ Then Jesus said to them, "Suppose you have a friend, and you go to him at midnight and say, 'Friend, lend me three loaves of bread; ⁶ a friend of mine on a journey has come to me, and I have no food to offer him.' ⁷ And suppose the one inside answers, 'Don't bother me. The door is already locked, and my children and I are in bed. I can't get up and give you anything.' ⁸ I tell you, even though he will not get up and give you the bread because of friendship, yet because of your shameless audacity he will surely get up and give you as much as you need.

⁹ "So I say to you: Ask and it will be given to you; seek and you will find; knock and the door will be opened to you. ¹⁰ For everyone who asks receives; the one who seeks finds; and to the one who knocks, the door will be opened.

¹¹ "Which of you fathers, if your son asks for a fish, will give him a snake instead? ¹² Or if he asks for an egg, will give him a scorpion? ¹³ If you then, though you are evil, know how to give good gifts to your children, how much more will your Father in heaven give the Holy Spirit to those who ask him!"

NEW KING JAMES VERSION

¹ Now it came to pass, as He was praying in a certain place, when He ceased, that one of His disciples said to Him, "Lord, teach us to pray, as John also taught his disciples."

² So He said to them, "When you pray, say:

Our Father in heaven,

Hallowed be Your name.

Your kingdom come.

Your will be done

On earth as it is in heaven.

³ Give us day by day our daily bread.

⁴ And forgive us our sins,

For we also forgive everyone who is indebted to us.

And do not lead us into temptation,

But deliver us from the evil one."

⁵ And He said to them, "Which of you shall have a friend, and go to him at midnight and say to him, 'Friend, lend me three loaves; ⁶ for a friend of mine has come to me on his journey, and I have nothing to set before him'; ⁷ and he will answer from within and say, 'Do not trouble me; the door is now shut, and my children are with me in bed; I cannot rise and give to you'? ⁸ I say to you, though he will not rise and give to him because he is his friend, yet because of his persistence he will rise and give him as many as he needs.

⁹ "So I say to you, ask, and it will be given to you; seek, and you will find; knock, and it will be opened to you. ¹⁰ For everyone who asks receives, and he who seeks finds, and to him who knocks it will be opened. ¹¹ If a son asks for bread from any father among you, will he give him a stone? Or if he asks for a fish, will he give him a serpent instead of a fish? ¹² Or if he asks for an egg, will he offer him a scorpion? ¹³ If you then, being evil, know how to give good gifts to your children, how much more will your heavenly Father give the Holy Spirit to those who ask Him!"

EXPLORATION

1. Why do you think Jesus' habit of prayer sparked the disciples' interest in prayer?

_____

_____

_____

_____

2. What do you notice about the model prayer Jesus gave to his disciples? In what ways is the similar or different from the way you typically pray?

_____

_____

_____

3. In Jesus' story of the friend in need of bread, whom do the two friends represent?

_____

_____

_____

4. What was Jesus saying about the need to be persistent in prayer? Why do you think God asks this of us?

_____

_____

_____

5. What spiritual principles did Jesus convey to his disciples through his daily example and teaching?

_____

_____

_____

6. What did Jesus say about the power his followers are given in prayer?

_____

_____

_____

INSPIRATION

The neighborhood is quiet. The streets are still. The sky is dark, and so is your friend's two-story house. But still you ring his doorbell, not once or twice but three times. Ding-dong. Ding-dong. Ding-dong. It's a big house, so it has a big chime. His Chihuahua wakes up. He has this snappy, who-do-you-think-you-are bark: "Ruff, ruff, ruff."

You envision what is happening upstairs. Your friend's wife is giving him a kick beneath the blankets. "Hank, get up! Someone is at the door." Poor guy. One minute sound asleep. The next, kicked out of bed. Doorbell ringing, dog barking. He's not going to like this.

The porch light comes on. The door opens. Boy, does he look like a mess. Boxer shorts. T-shirt. Bed hair. Face lined with pillow creases and covered in whiskers.

"What in the world are you doing here?" he asks.

"A friend of mine has just arrived for a visit, and I have nothing for him to eat," you answer.

The home owner grumbles and complains, but you insist. "Come on, Hank, please." Finally Hank acquiesces, invites you in, and takes you to his pantry. You fill a basket with food and take it home. And your surprise guest doesn't have to go to bed hungry. All because you spoke up on behalf of someone else.

This is intercessory prayer at its purest, a confluence of paucity and audacity. Father, you are good. They need help. I can't, but you can.

"I can't heal them, but, God, you can."

"I can't forgive them, but, God, you can."

"I can't help them, but, God, you can."

This prayer gets God's attention. After all, if Hank, a cranky, disgruntled friend, will help out, how much more will God do? He never sleeps. He's never irritated. When you knock on his door, he responds quickly and fairly. (From *Before Amen* by Max Lucado.)

REACTION

7. What does Jesus' story reveal about God's character?

_____

_____

_____

_____

_____

8. What does Jesus' story reveal about the way God responds to our prayers for others?

_____

_____

_____

_____

9. What are some steps you can take to keep your prayers honest and meaningful?

_____

_____

_____

_____

10. In what circumstances do you find it tempting to give up on praying for others?

_____

_____

_____

_____

11. What can be accomplished for God's kingdom through persistent prayer?

_____

_____

_____

_____

_____

12. In what way does this passage change your attitude toward a long-term prayer request or need in your life?

_____

_____

_____

_____

LIFE LESSONS

Jesus practiced a habit of prayer. Like any good habit, it must be deliberately maintained or it will fade away. God's faithfulness is often demonstrated in the Holy Spirit's gentle nudging and reminders to pray. Satan's craftiness is often demonstrated in mocking us when we fail to pray. We are always better off dwelling on God's reminders to pray than listening to our enemy's attempts to humiliate and discourage us. Persistence in prayer means going on despite any barriers or excuses not to do so.

DEVOTION

Father, forgive us for giving up on prayer so easily. Forgive us for our insincerity and lack of interest. We thank you for remaining faithful to us, even when we are unfaithful. Teach us how to pray honestly, persistently, and faithfully. Most importantly, Father, help us to follow in the footsteps of your perfect Son, Jesus Christ.

JOURNALING

What is one principle you can apply from this passage to strengthen your prayer life?

FOR FURTHER READING

To complete the book of Luke during this twelve-part study, read Luke 11:1–54. For more Bible passages on prayer, read 1 Chronicles 5:20; Matthew 17:20; 21:21–22; Luke 17:6; 18:40–42; Romans 12:12; Ephesians 6:18; James 5:15–16; and Jude 1:20.

LESSON EIGHT

TRUSTING GOD

"Therefore I tell you, do not worry about your life, what you will eat; or about your body, what you will wear."

LUKE 12:22

REFLECTION

Sometimes we make life harder than it needs to be. We rush around, working overtime to ensure we have all the things we want or need. In a consumer-oriented society, it's easy to miss Jesus' words about trusting in God. But Jesus said that God will meet our needs. Think about a time when God met one of your needs in an unexpected or unusual way. How did you know it was God working on your behalf?

_____

_____

_____

SITUATION

There are few scenes in the Gospels where crowds were not present. People loved to hear Jesus teach, and those who believed in him were transformed from being outsiders to being insiders in the kingdom of God. We are very much like them. As we read, we also "listen in" to conversations that Jesus had with his followers. Each time we do, we make some decisions about how we are going to accept Jesus' teaching. In this passage, Jesus offers an amazing teaching about lilies and birds and the kingdom.

OBSERVATION

Read Luke 12:22–34 from the New International Version or the New King James Version.

NEW INTERNATIONAL VERSION

²² Then Jesus said to his disciples: "Therefore I tell you, do not worry about your life, what you will eat; or about your body, what you will

wear. [23] For life is more than food, and the body more than clothes. [24] Consider the ravens: They do not sow or reap, they have no storeroom or barn; yet God feeds them. And how much more valuable you are than birds! [25] Who of you by worrying can add a single hour to your life? [26] Since you cannot do this very little thing, why do you worry about the rest?

[27] "Consider how the wild flowers grow. They do not labor or spin. Yet I tell you, not even Solomon in all his splendor was dressed like one of these. [28] If that is how God clothes the grass of the field, which is here today, and tomorrow is thrown into the fire, how much more will he clothe you—you of little faith! [29] And do not set your heart on what you will eat or drink; do not worry about it. [30] For the pagan world runs after all such things, and your Father knows that you need them. [31] But seek his kingdom, and these things will be given to you as well.

[32] "Do not be afraid, little flock, for your Father has been pleased to give you the kingdom. [33] Sell your possessions and give to the poor. Provide purses for yourselves that will not wear out, a treasure in heaven that will never fail, where no thief comes near and no moth destroys. [34] For where your treasure is, there your heart will be also.

New King James Version

[22] Then He said to His disciples, "Therefore I say to you, do not worry about your life, what you will eat; nor about the body, what you will put on. [23] Life is more than food, and the body is more than clothing. [24] Consider the ravens, for they neither sow nor reap, which have neither storehouse nor barn; and God feeds them. Of how much more value are you than the birds? [25] And which of you by worrying can add one cubit to his stature? [26] If you then are not able to do the least, why are you anxious for the rest? [27] Consider the lilies, how they grow: they neither toil nor spin; and yet I say to you, even Solomon in all his glory was not arrayed like one of these. [28] If then God so clothes the grass, which today is in the field and tomorrow is thrown into the oven, how much more will He clothe you, O you of little faith?

²⁹ "And do not seek what you should eat or what you should drink, nor have an anxious mind. ³⁰ For all these things the nations of the world seek after, and your Father knows that you need these things. ³¹ But seek the kingdom of God, and all these things shall be added to you.

³² "Do not fear, little flock, for it is your Father's good pleasure to give you the kingdom. ³³ Sell what you have and give alms; provide yourselves money bags which do not grow old, a treasure in the heavens that does not fail, where no thief approaches nor moth destroys. ³⁴ For where your treasure is, there your heart will be also.

EXPLORATION

1. What are some of the needs people have that Jesus said we should trust God to meet?

_____

_____

_____

_____

2. What point was Jesus making about how God provides for our food when he asked the disciples to "consider the ravens" (verse 24)?

_____

_____

_____

_____

3. What point was Jesus making about how God provides for our clothing when he asked the disciples to "consider how the wild flowers grow" (verse 27)?

_____

_____

_____

_____

4. In what ways does worry demonstrate a lack of faith in God?

_____

_____

_____

5. What are the rewards of seeking God's kingdom instead of personal gain?

_____

_____

_____

6. How do earthly riches differ from heavenly treasure? What does it mean to seek "treasure in heaven" (verse 33)?

_____

_____

_____

INSPIRATION

Do you really want the world to revolve around you? If it's all about you, then it's all up to you. Your Father rescues you from such a burden. While you are valuable, you aren't essential. You're important but not indispensable. Still don't think that's good news?

Perhaps a story would be helpful. My father, an oil-field mechanic, never met a car he couldn't fix. Forget golf clubs or tennis rackets, my dad's toys were sockets and wrenches. He relished a wrecked engine.... Dad did with a V-8 engine what Patton did with a platoon—he made it work.

Oh that the same could be said for his youngest son. It can't. My problem with mechanics begins with the ends of the car. I can't remember which one holds the engine. Anyone who confuses the spare tire with the fan belt is likely not gifted in car repair.

My ignorance left my dad in a precarious position. What does a skilled mechanic do with a son who is anything but? As you begin formulating an answer, may I ask this question: *What does God do with us?* Under his care the universe runs like a Rolex. But his children? Most of us have trouble balancing a checkbook. So what does he do?

I know what my dad did. Much to his credit, he let me help him. He gave me jobs to do—holding wrenches, scrubbing spark plugs. And he knew my limits. Never once did he say, "Max, tear apart that transmission, will you? One of the gears is broken." Never said it. For one thing, he liked his transmission. For another, he loved me. He loved me too much to give me too much.

So does God. He knows your limitations. He's well aware of your weaknesses. You can no more die for your own sins than you can solve world hunger. And, according to him, that's okay. The world doesn't rely on you . . . We don't know what it takes to run the world, and wise are we who leave the work to his hands. To say "It's not about you" is not to say you aren't loved; quite the contrary. It's because God loves you that it's not about you. (From *It's Not About Me* by Max Lucado.)

REACTION

7. What are some ways that God demonstrates he is taking care of you every day?

_____

_____

_____

_____

8. What are some of the consequences of anxiety? How can you avoid it?

_____

_____

_____

_____

9. Jesus says that God has given you the kingdom. How should this affect your attitude when you are facing difficult situations?

_____

_____

_____

_____

10. What is the difference between planning ahead and worrying?

_____

_____

_____

11. How does helping those in need demonstrate that your "treasure" is in the right place?

_____

_____

_____

_____

12. How has this passage inspired you to trust God with *all* your needs?

_____

_____

_____

LIFE LESSONS

This passage contains two valuable examples from which we can learn: *birds* and *lilies*. As we look at birds flit around, pecking out their daily survival, it reminds us of the countless details that God provides each day for our survival—things that we often take for granted. As we consider the lilies, we notice that rather than flying around and working to have their needs met, they sit still, and soak in what God sends. Lilies remind us of all the added benefits that God brings into our lives. Far more than the mere basics, God pours out blessings uncounted on our heads. Somewhere between bird-watching and the lily-considering, our worries disappear.

DEVOTION

Father, you have promised to protect and provide for your people. Forgive us for the times we choose to worry instead of depend on you. Help us see the futility of worry and the benefits of trusting you. Calm our fears and fill us with faith so we can focus our attention and energy on seeking your kingdom.

JOURNALING

When is it most difficult for you to trust God? Why at those particular times?

_____

_____

_____

_____

_____

_____

_____

_____

_____

FOR FURTHER READING

To complete the book of Luke during this twelve-part study, read Luke 12:1–14:35. For more Bible passages on trusting God, see Psalms 20:7; 37:3–5; 40:3–4; 125:1; Isaiah 26:4; Jeremiah 17:5–8; Nahum 1:7; Zephaniah 3:12; and Romans 9:33.

GOD'S LOVE FOR PEOPLE

*"Let us eat and be merry; for this my son was dead
and is alive again; he was lost and is found."*
LUKE 15:23–24 NKJV

REFLECTION

At some point in life, God's love must move from being a concept we wonder about to a conscious experience that transforms our lives. God's love deserves better than a half-hearted acknowledgment! In what tangible ways have you already felt God's love for you? In what ways has that love transformed your life?

SITUATION

Since the beginning of his ministry, Jesus had been traveling resolutely toward Jerusalem. The showdown with the Jewish religious leaders was coming. As he traveled, he continued to teach and heal. Desperate people came to him, and he welcomed them, much to the dismay and anger of his enemies. Yet instead of arguing directly with his opponents or pointing out their hypocrisy in plain language, Jesus resorted to parables. These short stories invited questions and provoked pondering. They also contained a barb of truth that prodded the deceitful while at the same time communicated God's great love for sinners.

OBSERVATION

*Read Luke 15:11–32 from the New International
Version or the New King James Version.*

NEW INTERNATIONAL VERSION
¹¹ Jesus continued: "There was a man who had two sons. ¹² The younger one said to his father, 'Father, give me my share of the estate.' So he divided his property between them.

[13] "Not long after that, the younger son got together all he had, set off for a distant country and there squandered his wealth in wild living. [14] After he had spent everything, there was a severe famine in that whole country, and he began to be in need. [15] So he went and hired himself out to a citizen of that country, who sent him to his fields to feed pigs. [16] He longed to fill his stomach with the pods that the pigs were eating, but no one gave him anything.

[17] "When he came to his senses, he said, 'How many of my father's hired servants have food to spare, and here I am starving to death! [18] I will set out and go back to my father and say to him: Father, I have sinned against heaven and against you.[19] I am no longer worthy to be called your son; make me like one of your hired servants.' [20] So he got up and went to his father.

"But while he was still a long way off, his father saw him and was filled with compassion for him; he ran to his son, threw his arms around him and kissed him.

[21] "The son said to him, 'Father, I have sinned against heaven and against you. I am no longer worthy to be called your son.'

[22] "But the father said to his servants, 'Quick! Bring the best robe and put it on him. Put a ring on his finger and sandals on his feet. [23] Bring the fattened calf and kill it. Let's have a feast and celebrate. [24] For this son of mine was dead and is alive again; he was lost and is found.' So they began to celebrate.

[25] "Meanwhile, the older son was in the field. When he came near the house, he heard music and dancing. [26] So he called one of the servants and asked him what was going on. [27] 'Your brother has come,' he replied, 'and your father has killed the fattened calf because he has him back safe and sound.'

[28] "The older brother became angry and refused to go in. So his father went out and pleaded with him. [29] But he answered his father, 'Look! All these years I've been slaving for you and never disobeyed your orders. Yet you never gave me even a young goat so I could celebrate with my friends. [30] But when this son of yours who has squandered your property with prostitutes comes home, you kill the fattened calf for him!'

³¹ "'My son,' the father said, 'you are always with me, and everything I have is yours. ³² But we had to celebrate and be glad, because this brother of yours was dead and is alive again; he was lost and is found.'"

NEW KING JAMES VERSION

¹¹ Then He said: "A certain man had two sons. ¹² And the younger of them said to his father, 'Father, give me the portion of goods that falls to me.' So he divided to them his livelihood. ¹³ And not many days after, the younger son gathered all together, journeyed to a far country, and there wasted his possessions with prodigal living. ¹⁴ But when he had spent all, there arose a severe famine in that land, and he began to be in want. ¹⁵ Then he went and joined himself to a citizen of that country, and he sent him into his fields to feed swine. ¹⁶ And he would gladly have filled his stomach with the pods that the swine ate, and no one gave him anything.

¹⁷ "But when he came to himself, he said, 'How many of my father's hired servants have bread enough and to spare, and I perish with hunger! ¹⁸ I will arise and go to my father, and will say to him, "Father, I have sinned against heaven and before you, ¹⁹ and I am no longer worthy to be called your son. Make me like one of your hired servants."'

²⁰ "And he arose and came to his father. But when he was still a great way off, his father saw him and had compassion, and ran and fell on his neck and kissed him. ²¹ And the son said to him, 'Father, I have sinned against heaven and in your sight, and am no longer worthy to be called your son.'

²² "But the father said to his servants, 'Bring out the best robe and put it on him, and put a ring on his hand and sandals on his feet. ²³ And bring the fatted calf here and kill it, and let us eat and be merry; ²⁴ for this my son was dead and is alive again; he was lost and is found.' And they began to be merry.

²⁵ "Now his older son was in the field. And as he came and drew near to the house, he heard music and dancing. ²⁶ So he called one of the servants and asked what these things meant. ²⁷ And he said to him, 'Your

brother has come, and because he has received him safe and sound, your father has killed the fatted calf.'

[28] "But he was angry and would not go in. Therefore his father came out and pleaded with him. [29] So he answered and said to his father, 'Lo, these many years I have been serving you; I never transgressed your commandment at any time; and yet you never gave me a young goat, that I might make merry with my friends.[30] But as soon as this son of yours came, who has devoured your livelihood with harlots, you killed the fatted calf for him.'

[31] "And he said to him, 'Son, you are always with me, and all that I have is yours.[32] It was right that we should make merry and be glad, for your brother was dead and is alive again, and was lost and is found.'"

EXPLORATION

1. Who were the three characters in Jesus' parable? Who did they each represent?

_____

_____

_____

_____

2. What character traits of God are highlighted in the parable?

_____

_____

_____

_____

3. What happens when God gives people freedom to make their own choices?

_____

_____

_____

4. In what ways have you, like the younger son, showed disregard for God's authority?

_____

_____

_____

5. In what ways have you, like the older son, showed disregard for God's mercy toward others?

_____

_____

_____

6. In what way does God respond to people who confess their sins and return to him?

_____

_____

_____

INSPIRATION

Captured in the portrait is a tender scene of a father and a son. Behind them is a great house on a hill. Beneath their feet is a narrow path. Down from the house the father has run. Up the trail the son has trudged. The two have met, here, at the gate.

We can't see the face of the son; it's buried in the chest of his father. We can see the mud on the back of his legs, the filth on his shoulders and the empty purse on the ground. At one time the purse was full of money. At one time the boy was full of pride. But that was a dozen taverns ago. Now both the purse and the pride are depleted.

The prodigal offers no gift or explanation. All he offers is the smell of pigs and a rehearsed apology. He feels unworthy of his birthright. . . . The boy is content to be a hired hand. There is only one problem. Though the boy is willing to stop being a son, the father is not willing to stop being a father.

Look at the tears glistening on the father's leathered cheeks, the smile shining through the silver beard. One arm holds the boy up so he won't fall, the other holds the boy close so he won't doubt. "Quick!" he shouts. "Bring the best robe and put it on him. Put a ring on his finger and sandals on his feet. Bring the fattened calf and kill it. Let's have a feast and celebrate. For this son of mine was dead and is alive again; he was lost and is found" (Luke 15:22–24).

How these words must have stunned the young man. "*This son of mine* was dead . . ." He thought he'd lost his place in the home. After all, didn't he abandon his father? Didn't he waste his inheritance? The boy assumed he had forfeited his privilege to sonship. The father, however, doesn't give up that easily. In his mind, his son is still a son. The child may have been out of the house, but he was never out of his father's heart. He may have left the table, but he never left the family.

Don't miss the message here. You may be willing to stop being God's child. But God is not willing to stop being your Father. (From *The Great House of God* by Max Lucado.)

REACTION

7. Why is it important to recognize that God values all people equally?

_____

_____

_____

8. How does it feel to know that God sees *all* of your faults and still loves you?

_____

_____

_____

9. Why do you think God allows difficult times in your life like the prodigal son experienced?

_____

_____

_____

10. What does this parable tell you about the way God forgives you?

_____

_____

_____

11. What does this parable tell you about recognizing all the blessings God has given to you as his child? How should that compel you to be merciful to others?

_____

_____

_____

12. Think of one person you know who is difficult to love. In what ways can you show God's love to that person?

_____

_____

_____

LIFE LESSONS

Parent, sibling, and wayward child—all of us relate in one way or another to the parable that Jesus told. Often we play more than one part, and each of the parts enables us to learn something about love. God designed relationships in such a way that allows us the opportunity to love and be loved. Some people will disappoint us, and we will disappoint others . . . only God loves perfectly. But he will help us to love better than we could possibly accomplish in our own strength. In fact, "We love because he first loved us" (1 John 4:19).

DEVOTION

We stand in awe, Father, of your great love—a love so deep that you sacrificed your only Son to save us. Forgive us for our rebellion and disobedience. Give us the strength to turn away from our sin and accept your forgiveness. And help us see others through your loving eyes.

JOURNALING

How will you thank God for treating you better than you deserve?

FOR FURTHER READING

To complete the book of Luke during this twelve-part study, read Luke 15:1–18:43. For more Bible passages on God's love for us, read Deuteronomy 7:8; Jeremiah 31:3; John 3:16; Romans 5:8; Ephesians 2:4–5; and 1 John 3:1; 4:7–21.

TRUE WORSHIP

*When Jesus entered the temple courts, he began to
drive out those who were selling. "It is written," he
said to them, "'My house will be a house of prayer';
but you have made it 'a den of robbers.'"*
LUKE 19:45–46

REFLECTION

When celebrities arrive at a gala event, they are greeted with applause, red carpet treatment, and a dizzying barrage of camera flashes. On more formal occasions, the chaos is replaced with hushed tones and whispered comments. When someone important arrives on the scene, others pay attention. If Jesus were to visit your church, how do you think he would be greeted? Do you think he would feel comfortable? Would he be noticed?

_____

_____

_____

_____

_____

SITUATION

Countless people were making their way into David's city, Jerusalem, for the yearly celebration of the Passover. In a symbolic gesture, Jesus rode a colt into town, re-enacting an ancient tradition of a king coming in peace. He was greeted with praise and palm branches, but as he approached the city he wept over it, for he knew the people would ultimately reject him.

OBSERVATION

Read Luke 19:37–48 from the New International Version or the New King James Version.

NEW INTERNATIONAL VERSION

³⁷ When he came near the place where the road goes down the Mount of Olives, the whole crowd of disciples began joyfully to praise God in loud voices for all the miracles they had seen:

³⁸ "Blessed is the king who comes in the name of the Lord!"

"Peace in heaven and glory in the highest!"

³⁹ Some of the Pharisees in the crowd said to Jesus, "Teacher, rebuke your disciples!"

⁴⁰ "I tell you," he replied, "if they keep quiet, the stones will cry out."

⁴¹ As he approached Jerusalem and saw the city, he wept over it ⁴² and said, "If you, even you, had only known on this day what would bring you peace—but now it is hidden from your eyes. ⁴³ The days will come upon you when your enemies will build an embankment against you and encircle you and hem you in on every side. ⁴⁴ They will dash you to the ground, you and the children within your walls. They will not leave one stone on another, because you did not recognize the time of God's coming to you."

⁴⁵ When Jesus entered the temple courts, he began to drive out those who were selling. ⁴⁶ "It is written," he said to them, "'My house will be a house of prayer'; but you have made it 'a den of robbers.'"

⁴⁷ Every day he was teaching at the temple. But the chief priests, the teachers of the law and the leaders among the people were trying to kill him. ⁴⁸ Yet they could not find any way to do it, because all the people hung on his words.

New King James Version

³⁷ Then, as He was now drawing near the descent of the Mount of Olives, the whole multitude of the disciples began to rejoice and praise God with a loud voice for all the mighty works they had seen, ³⁸ saying:

"'Blessed is the King who comes in the name of the Lord!'
Peace in heaven and glory in the highest!"

³⁹ And some of the Pharisees called to Him from the crowd, "Teacher, rebuke Your disciples."

⁴⁰ But He answered and said to them, "I tell you that if these should keep silent, the stones would immediately cry out."

[41] Now as He drew near, He saw the city and wept over it, [42] saying, "If you had known, even you, especially in this your day, the things that make for your peace! But now they are hidden from your eyes. [43] For days will come upon you when your enemies will build an embankment around you, surround you and close you in on every side, [44] and level you, and your children within you, to the ground; and they will not leave in you one stone upon another, because you did not know the time of your visitation."

[45] Then He went into the temple and began to drive out those who bought and sold in it, [46] saying to them, "It is written, 'My house is a house of prayer,' but you have made it a 'den of thieves.'"

[47] And He was teaching daily in the temple. But the chief priests, the scribes, and the leaders of the people sought to destroy Him, [48] and were unable to do anything; for all the people were very attentive to hear Him.

EXPLORATION

1. Why did the people celebrate Jesus' entrance into Jerusalem?

_____

_____

_____

_____

_____

_____

2. How did the Pharisees react to the crowds? How did Jesus respond to them?

_____

_____

_____

_____

_____

3. Why did Jesus weep when he saw Jerusalem, while all the people were praising him?

_____

_____

_____

4. Why did Jesus not tolerate the buying and selling in the temple?

_____

_____

_____

5. Jesus called the temple "a house of prayer." How well does that describe our churches today?

_____

_____

_____

6. What message did Jesus send to church leaders when he cleared the temple?

_____

_____

_____

INSPIRATION

It's a sad but true fact of the faith: religion is used for profit and prestige. When it is, there are two results: people are exploited and God is infuriated. There's no better example of this than what happened at the temple.... What did Jesus see? Hucksters. Faith peddlers. People in the temple making a franchise out of the faith.

It was Passover week. The Passover was the highlight of the Jewish calendar. People came from all regions and many countries to be present for the celebration. Upon arriving they were obligated to meet two requirements. First, an animal sacrifice, usually a dove. The dove had to be perfect, without blemish. . . . So, under the guise of keeping the sacrifice pure, the dove sellers sold doves—at their price. Second, the people had to pay a temple tax . . . in local currency.

Knowing many foreigners would be in Jerusalem to pay the tax, money changers conveniently set up tables and offered to exchange the foreign money for local— for a modest fee, of course.

It's not difficult to see what angered Jesus. Pilgrims journeyed days to see God, to witness the holy, to worship His Majesty. But before they were taken into the presence of God, they were taken to the cleaners. . . .

"I've had enough," was written all over the Messiah's face. In he stormed. Doves flapped and tables flew. People scampered and traders scattered. This was not an impulsive show. This was not a temper tantrum. It was a deliberate act with an intentional message . . . Knowing his days were drawing to a close, he chose to make a point: God will never hold guiltless those who exploit the privilege of worship. (From *And the Angels Were Silent* by Max Lucado.)

REACTION

7. How would you define true worship of God?

_____

_____

_____

8. What are some things that can interfere with your worship?

_____

_____

_____

9. How can you determine whether your motives are pure when you go to church?

_____

_____

_____

10. What are some ways people misuse religion for their own purposes?

_____

_____

11. What responsibility do you have to eliminate inappropriate activities and behavior from the church?

_____

_____

_____

12. What steps can believers take to protect the church from exploitation?

_____

_____

LIFE LESSONS

Worship takes on a different tone when we stop long enough to remember that Jesus sees more than external actions. Our attempts at going through the motions may impress others and satisfy our own ideas of what "minimum worship requirements" involves, but God sees our hearts, our intentions, and the flow of our thoughts. Although much attention is given to worship styles—contemporary versus traditional, spontaneous versus liturgical—these concerns pale before the ultimate issue of what God witnesses when we worship. We have God's attention when we enter worship. What will we do with it?

DEVOTION

Father, forgive us for our insincerity and dishonesty. We want to learn how to worship you in spirit and in truth. We need you, Father, to help us witness your holiness, bask in your glory, and feel your presence. May we truly be thankful for the privilege of worshipping you.

JOURNALING

In light of this passage, what changes do you need to make in the way you approach worship?

_____

_____

_____

_____

_____

_____

_____

_____

_____

_____

_____

_____

FOR FURTHER READING

To complete the book of Luke during this twelve-part study, read Luke 19:1–20:47. For more Bible passages on worship, read Joshua 22:27; 1 Chronicles 16:28–29; 2 Chronicles 29:30; Psalm 95:6; Zechariah 14:17; Matthew 2:2; John 4:24; and Romans 12:1.

CHRIST'S SACRIFICE

Then the sun was darkened, and the veil of the temple was torn in two. And when Jesus had cried out with a loud voice, He said, "Father, 'into Your hands I commit My spirit.'" Having said this, He breathed His last.

LUKE 23:45–46 NKJV

REFLECTION

A sacrifice should be just that—a sacrifice. Sacrifices may be inconvenient and are costly. By definition, a sacrifice almost always involves some kind of death or loss. Think of a time when you gave something up for a friend. In what way did your sacrifice help that person?

SITUATION

Shortly after Jesus drove out the merchants in the temple, the religious leaders convinced Judas, one of Jesus' own disciples, to betray him. Sham trials followed, a guilty verdict was passed, and soon the Roman soldiers were forcing Jesus to make his way to the place of execution. The details Luke goes on to relate in his account—a passerby recruited to help carry the cross, women watching and weeping, two other death-row criminals almost forgotten in the crowd, a mocking sign—all create a haunting scene of sacrifice.

OBSERVATION

Read Luke 23:26–49 from the New International Version or the New King James Version.

NEW INTERNATIONAL VERSION

26 As the soldiers led him away, they seized Simon from Cyrene, who was on his way in from the country, and put the cross on him and made him carry it behind Jesus. 27 A large number of people followed him, including women who mourned and wailed for him. 28 Jesus turned and

said to them, "Daughters of Jerusalem, do not weep for me; weep for yourselves and for your children. ²⁹ For the time will come when you will say, 'Blessed are the childless women, the wombs that never bore and the breasts that never nursed!' ³⁰ Then

> "'they will say to the mountains, "Fall on us!"
> and to the hills, "Cover us!"'

³¹ For if people do these things when the tree is green, what will happen when it is dry?"

³² Two other men, both criminals, were also led out with him to be executed.³³ When they came to the place called the Skull, they crucified him there, along with the criminals—one on his right, the other on his left. ³⁴ Jesus said, "Father, forgive them, for they do not know what they are doing." And they divided up his clothes by casting lots.

³⁵ The people stood watching, and the rulers even sneered at him. They said, "He saved others; let him save himself if he is God's Messiah, the Chosen One."

³⁶ The soldiers also came up and mocked him. They offered him wine vinegar³⁷ and said, "If you are the king of the Jews, save yourself."

³⁸ There was a written notice above him, which read: THIS IS THE KING OF THE JEWS.

³⁹ One of the criminals who hung there hurled insults at him: "Aren't you the Messiah? Save yourself and us!"

⁴⁰ But the other criminal rebuked him. "Don't you fear God," he said, "since you are under the same sentence? ⁴¹ We are punished justly, for we are getting what our deeds deserve. But this man has done nothing wrong."

⁴² Then he said, "Jesus, remember me when you come into your kingdom."

⁴³ Jesus answered him, "Truly I tell you, today you will be with me in paradise."

⁴⁴ It was now about noon, and darkness came over the whole land until three in the afternoon, ⁴⁵ for the sun stopped shining. And the

curtain of the temple was torn in two. ⁴⁶ Jesus called out with a loud voice, "Father, into your hands I commit my spirit." When he had said this, he breathed his last.

⁴⁷ The centurion, seeing what had happened, praised God and said, "Surely this was a righteous man." ⁴⁸ When all the people who had gathered to witness this sight saw what took place, they beat their breasts and went away. ⁴⁹ But all those who knew him, including the women who had followed him from Galilee, stood at a distance, watching these things.

New King James Version

²⁶ Now as they led Him away, they laid hold of a certain man, Simon a Cyrenian, who was coming from the country, and on him they laid the cross that he might bear it after Jesus.

²⁷ And a great multitude of the people followed Him, and women who also mourned and lamented Him. ²⁸ But Jesus, turning to them, said, "Daughters of Jerusalem, do not weep for Me, but weep for yourselves and for your children.²⁹ For indeed the days are coming in which they will say, 'Blessed are the barren, wombs that never bore, and breasts which never nursed!' ³⁰ Then they will begin 'to say to the mountains, "Fall on us!" and to the hills, "Cover us!"' ³¹ For if they do these things in the green wood, what will be done in the dry?"

³² There were also two others, criminals, led with Him to be put to death. ³³ And when they had come to the place called Calvary, there they crucified Him, and the criminals, one on the right hand and the other on the left. ³⁴ Then Jesus said, "Father, forgive them, for they do not know what they do."

And they divided His garments and cast lots. ³⁵ And the people stood looking on. But even the rulers with them sneered, saying, "He saved others; let Him save Himself if He is the Christ, the chosen of God."

³⁶ The soldiers also mocked Him, coming and offering Him sour wine, ³⁷ and saying, "If You are the King of the Jews, save Yourself."

³⁸ And an inscription also was written over Him in letters of Greek, Latin, and Hebrew:

THIS IS THE KING OF THE JEWS.

[39] Then one of the criminals who were hanged blasphemed Him, saying, "If You are the Christ, save Yourself and us."

[40] But the other, answering, rebuked him, saying, "Do you not even fear God, seeing you are under the same condemnation? [41] And we indeed justly, for we receive the due reward of our deeds; but this Man has done nothing wrong." [42] Then he said to Jesus, "Lord, remember me when You come into Your kingdom."

[43] And Jesus said to him, "Assuredly, I say to you, today you will be with Me in Paradise."

[44] Now it was about the sixth hour, and there was darkness over all the earth until the ninth hour. [45] Then the sun was darkened, and the veil of the temple was torn in two. [46] And when Jesus had cried out with a loud voice, He said, "Father, 'into Your hands I commit My spirit.'" Having said this, He breathed His last.

[47] So when the centurion saw what had happened, he glorified God, saying, "Certainly this was a righteous Man!"

[48] And the whole crowd who came together to that sight, seeing what had been done, beat their breasts and returned. [49] But all His acquaintances, and the women who followed Him from Galilee, stood at a distance, watching these things.

EXPLORATION

1. What character traits did Jesus exhibit during the hours before his death?

_____

_____

_____

_____

_____

2. How did Jesus show mercy to the people who were executing him? To the criminal who asked Jesus to remember him when he entered into his kingdom?

3. In what ways should believers try to imitate Christ's attitude of forgiveness?

4. What was the significance at the time of Christ's death of the torn curtain in the temple leading into the Holy of Holies?

5. Why did Jesus submit to God's plan of salvation for the world?

6. Why was Jesus' sacrifice necessary to restore the relationship between God and humans?

INSPIRATION

The King looked at the Prince of Light. "The darkness will be great." He passed his hand over the spotless face of his Son. "The pain will be awful." Then he paused and looked at his darkened dominion. When he looked up, his eyes were moist. "But there is no other way."

The Son looked into the stars as he heard the answer. "Then, let it be done." Slowly the words that would kill the Son began to come from the lips of the Father.

"Hour of death, moment of sacrifice, it is your moment. Rehearsed a million times on false altars with false lambs; the moment of truth has come. . . .

"Soldiers, you think you lead him? Ropes, you think you bind him? Men, you think you sentence him? He heeds not your commands. He winces not at your lashes. It is my voice he obeys. It is my condemnation he dreads. And it is your souls he saves.

"Oh, my Son, my Child. Look up into the heavens and see my face before I turn it. Hear my voice before I silence it. Would that I could save you and them. But they don't see and they don't hear.

"The living must die so that the dying can live. The time has come to kill the Lamb.". . .

God must have wept as he performed his task. Every lie, every lure, every act done in shadows was in that cup. Slowly, hideously they were absorbed into the body of the Son. The final act of incarnation. . . .

The throne room is dark and cavernous. The eyes of the King are closed. He is resting.

In his dream he is again in the Garden. The cool of the evening floats across the river as the three walk. They speak of the Garden—of how it is, of how it will be.

"Father . . ." the Son begins. The King replays the word again. *Father. Father.* The word was a flower, petal-delicate, yet so easily crushed. Oh, how he longed for his children to call him Father again.

A noise snaps him from his dream. He opens his eyes and sees a transcendent figure gleaming in the doorway. "It is finished, Father. I have come home." (From *Six Hours One Friday* by Max Lucado.)

REACTION

7. How would you explain the significance of Jesus' death on the cross?

_____

_____

_____

_____

8. Why is it important to accept Christ's sacrifice on your behalf?

_____

_____

_____

_____

9. For what reasons do people refuse God's gift of salvation?

_____

_____

_____

_____

10. How would your life be different if Jesus had never died and risen again?

_____

_____

_____

_____

11. How do you feel when you think about the pain and anguish Jesus endured for you?

_____

_____

_____

_____

12. Who is one person you can tell about Christ's work on the cross?

_____

_____

_____

_____

LIFE LESSONS

The Gospel accounts make it clear that Jesus went to the cross _willingly_. He did not die because others were stronger than him or because he deserved the treatment he received. He had a reason for surrendering his life beyond the immediate circumstances. His prayer from the cross for his executioners to be forgiven should to pluck a chord in us—for as sinners, we share in the cause of his death. His promise of paradise to the repentant criminal ought to cause our hearts to leap and our lips to whisper, "Me too, Lord!" Does it? Personally owning Christ's death is the most valuable life lesson we could ever learn. Not only is it priceless . . . it is also eternal.

DEVOTION

Lord, you were willing to suffer pain, ridicule, and even death for us. How can we ever thank you? All we can offer you is our hearts and lives. Help us to love and obey you until we meet face-to-face in heaven. And while we wait for that day, use us to bring others into a right relationship with you.

JOURNALING

How can you show your appreciation for what Jesus has done for you?

_____

_____

_____

_____

_____

_____

_____

_____

_____

_____

_____

_____

_____

_____

_____

_____

_____

_____

FOR FURTHER READING

To complete the book of Luke during this twelve-part study, read Luke
21:1– 23:56. For more Bible passages on Jesus' sacrifice, read Romans
3:23–26; 8:32; Galatians 2:20; 1 Timothy 2:5–6; Titus 2:12–14; Hebrews
7:27; 9:23–28; 10:9–18; and 1 John 2:1–2; 4:10.

LESSON TWELVE

SEEING JESUS

*Then their eyes were opened and they recognized him, and
he disappeared from their sight. They asked each other,
"Were not our hearts burning within us while he talked
with us on the road and opened the Scriptures to us?"*
LUKE 24:31–32

REFLECTION

If you know Jesus personally, it is likely that someone introduced him to you. Perhaps many people were involved in your coming to faith. Take a few minutes to think about the people through whom God worked to communicate his message of love to you. Who helped you understand your need for a relationship with Jesus? How did they do this?

SITUATION

Luke tells us that on the first day of the week, several women went to Jesus' tomb but found it empty. As they stood wondering about this, two angels appeared and told them that Jesus had risen from the dead. The news spread like wildfire . . . though Jesus' followers had a hard time accepting it. Two believers left Jerusalem and headed to Emmaus. As they walked and talked, another man joined them—a man who asked interesting questions and seemed curiously ignorant of the recent events. The travelers were amazed at how much the stranger knew about Jesus and the ancient Scriptures. His companionship was so warm they couldn't resist inviting him to stay with them for the evening. That's when their eyes were really opened.

OBSERVATION

Read Luke 24:13–35 from the New International
Version or the New King James Version.

New International Version

¹³ Now that same day two of them were going to a village called Emmaus, about seven miles from Jerusalem. ¹⁴ They were talking with each other about everything that had happened. ¹⁵ As they talked and discussed these things with each other, Jesus himself came up and walked along with them; ¹⁶ but they were kept from recognizing him.

¹⁷ He asked them, "What are you discussing together as you walk along?"

They stood still, their faces downcast. ¹⁸ One of them, named Cleopas, asked him, "Are you the only one visiting Jerusalem who does not know the things that have happened there in these days?"

¹⁹ "What things?" he asked.

"About Jesus of Nazareth," they replied. "He was a prophet, powerful in word and deed before God and all the people. ²⁰ The chief priests and our rulers handed him over to be sentenced to death, and they crucified him; ²¹ but we had hoped that he was the one who was going to redeem Israel. And what is more, it is the third day since all this took place. ²² In addition, some of our women amazed us. They went to the tomb early this morning ²³ but didn't find his body. They came and told us that they had seen a vision of angels, who said he was alive. ²⁴ Then some of our companions went to the tomb and found it just as the women had said, but they did not see Jesus."

²⁵ He said to them, "How foolish you are, and how slow to believe all that the prophets have spoken! ²⁶ Did not the Messiah have to suffer these things and then enter his glory?" ²⁷ And beginning with Moses and all the Prophets, he explained to them what was said in all the Scriptures concerning himself.

²⁸ As they approached the village to which they were going, Jesus continued on as if he were going farther. ²⁹ But they urged him strongly,

"Stay with us, for it is nearly evening; the day is almost over." So he went in to stay with them.

³⁰ When he was at the table with them, he took bread, gave thanks, broke it and began to give it to them. ³¹ Then their eyes were opened and they recognized him, and he disappeared from their sight. ³² They asked each other, "Were not our hearts burning within us while he talked with us on the road and opened the Scriptures to us?"

³³ They got up and returned at once to Jerusalem. There they found the Eleven and those with them, assembled together ³⁴ and saying, "It is true! The Lord has risen and has appeared to Simon." ³⁵ Then the two told what had happened on the way, and how Jesus was recognized by them when he broke the bread.

New King James Version

¹³ Now behold, two of them were traveling that same day to a village called Emmaus, which was seven miles from Jerusalem. ¹⁴ And they talked together of all these things which had happened. ¹⁵ So it was, while they conversed and reasoned, that Jesus Himself drew near and went with them. ¹⁶ But their eyes were restrained, so that they did not know Him.

¹⁷ And He said to them, "What kind of conversation is this that you have with one another as you walk and are sad?"

¹⁸ Then the one whose name was Cleopas answered and said to Him, "Are You the only stranger in Jerusalem, and have You not known the things which happened there in these days?"

¹⁹ And He said to them, "What things?"

So they said to Him, "The things concerning Jesus of Nazareth, who was a Prophet mighty in deed and word before God and all the people, ²⁰ and how the chief priests and our rulers delivered Him to be condemned to death, and crucified Him. ²¹ But we were hoping that it was He who was going to redeem Israel. Indeed, besides all this, today is the third day since these things happened. ²² Yes, and certain women of our company, who arrived at the tomb early, astonished us. ²³ When they did not find His body, they came saying that they had also seen a vision of angels who said He was alive. ²⁴ And certain of those who were with us went to the tomb and found it just as the women had said; but Him they did not see."

²⁵ Then He said to them, "O foolish ones, and slow of heart to believe in all that the prophets have spoken! ²⁶ Ought not the Christ to have suffered these things and to enter into His glory?" ²⁷ And beginning at Moses and all the Prophets, He expounded to them in all the Scriptures the things concerning Himself.

²⁸ Then they drew near to the village where they were going, and He indicated that He would have gone farther. ²⁹ But they constrained Him, saying, "Abide with us, for it is toward evening, and the day is far spent." And He went in to stay with them.

³⁰ Now it came to pass, as He sat at the table with them, that He took bread, blessed and broke it, and gave it to them. ³¹ Then their eyes were opened and they knew Him; and He vanished from their sight.

³² And they said to one another, "Did not our heart burn within us while He talked with us on the road, and while He opened the Scriptures to us?" ³³ So they rose up that very hour and returned to Jerusalem, and found the eleven and those who were with them gathered together, ³⁴ saying, "The Lord is risen indeed, and has appeared to Simon!" ³⁵ And they told about the things that had happened on the road, and how He was known to them in the breaking of bread.

EXPLORATION

1. What did the men say about Jesus? How did Jesus respond to them?

_____

_____

_____

2. Why do you think Jesus did not make himself known to the men?

_____

_____

_____

3. What did the men do after they realized Jesus had been in their midst?

_____

_____

_____

4. What prevents people today from recognizing Jesus as Savior?

_____

_____

_____

5. In what different ways does Jesus reveal himself to people today?

_____

_____

_____

6. What role does the Holy Spirit play in helping us see Jesus?

_____

_____

_____

INSPIRATION

Jesus. Have you seen him? Those who first did were never the same. "My Lord and my God!" cried Thomas.

"I have seen the Lord," exclaimed Mary Magdalene.

"We have seen his glory," declared John.

"Were not our hearts burning within us while he talked?" rejoiced the two Emmaus-bound disciples.

But Peter said it best. "We were eyewitnesses of his majesty."

His Majesty. The emperor of Judah. The soaring eagle of eternity. The noble admiral of the Kingdom. All the splendor of heaven revealed in a human body. For a period ever so brief, the doors to the throne room were open and God came near. His Majesty was seen. Heaven touched the earth and, as a result, earth can know heaven. In astounding tandem a human body housed divinity. Holiness and earthliness intertwined.

This is no run-of-the-mill messiah. His story was extraordinary. He called himself divine, yet allowed a minimum-wage Roman soldier to drive a nail into his wrist. He demanded purity, yet stood for the rights of a repentant whore. He called men to march, yet refused to allow them to call him King. He sent men into all the world, yet equipped them with only bended knees and memories of a resurrected carpenter.

We can't regard him as simply a good teacher. His claims are too outrageous to limit him to the company of Socrates or Aristotle. Nor can we categorize him as one of many prophets sent to reveal eternal truths. His own claims eliminate that possibility.

Has it been a while since you have seen him? If your prayers seem stale, it probably has. If your faith seems to be trembling, perhaps your vision of him has blurred. If you can't find power to face your problems, perhaps it is time to face him. (From *God Came Near* by Max Lucado.)

REACTION

7. In what way can meeting Jesus change a person's life?

_____

_____

_____

_____

8. What was your first encounter with Jesus? What enabled you to see him as the Messiah?

_____

_____

_____

_____

9. In what ways has your relationship with Jesus grown and matured?

_____

_____

_____

10. What are some ways that life's problems and disappointments interfere with our communion with God?

_____

_____

_____

11. What can believers do when God seems far away?

_____

_____

_____

12. What steps can you take to nurture your relationship with Jesus?

_____

_____

_____

LIFE LESSONS

Perhaps this study has turned into a "road to Emmaus" lesson for you. You thought you knew Jesus, but you've discovered there's a lot more to him than you realized. Only you can determine if this was the beginning of a relationship or the deepening of one. But you can be sure of this: even as Jesus made himself unexpectedly available and known to those disciples on the road, he will do the same for you. At times when you least expect him, he will show up and make a difference. Live your life _for_ him, and you will be delighted with how often you notice you're living _with_ him.

DEVOTION

Father, thank you for sending your Son to free us from the penalty of sin. Thank you that he rose from the dead and lives today. And thank you for giving us your Holy Spirit to help us recognize and accept Jesus as our Savior. Guide us into a deeper relationship with you, so that when we go through difficult times, we can run to you and rest secure in your presence. Thank you for showing up on our road of life, too.

JOURNALING

How has meeting Jesus had an impact on your life?

FOR FURTHER READING

To complete the book of Luke during this twelve-part study, read Luke 24:1–53. For more Bible passages on knowing Jesus, see John 10:14–27; Ephesians 1:15–17; Philippians 3:8–10; 2 Timothy 1:12; and 1 John 2:3–6, 29; 3:1–3; 4:13–16.

LEADER'S GUIDE FOR SMALL GROUPS

Thank you for your willingness to lead a group through *Life Lessons from Luke*. The rewards of being a leader are different from those of participating, and we hope you find your own walk with Jesus deepened by this experience. During the twelve lessons in this study, you will guide your group through selected passages in Luke and explore the key themes of the Gospel. There are several elements in this leader's guide that will help you as you structure your study and reflection time, so be sure to follow along and take advantage of each one.

BEFORE YOU BEGIN

Before your first meeting, make sure the group members have their own copy of the *Life Lessons from Luke* study guide so they can follow along and have their answers written out ahead of time. Alternately, you can hand out the guides at your first meeting and give the group some time to look over the material and ask any preliminary questions. Be sure to send a sheet around the room during that first meeting and have the members write down their name, phone number, and email address so you can keep in touch with them during the week.

There are several ways to structure the duration of the study. You can choose to cover each lesson individually for a total of twelve weeks of discussion, or you can combine two lessons together per week for a total of six weeks of discussion. You can also choose to have the group members read just the selected passages of Scripture given in each lesson, or they can cover the entire book of Luke by reading the material listed in the "For Further Reading" section at the end of each lesson. The following table illustrates these options:

Twelve-Week Format

Week	Lessons Covered	Simplified Reading	Expanded Reading
1	Hope in God	Luke 1:5–25	Luke 1:1–3:38
2	Faith at Work	Luke 5:17–26	Luke 4:1–5:39
3	A New Standard	Luke 6:1–11	Luke 6:1–49
4	Christ's Compassion	Luke 7:11–23	Luke 7:1–50
5	Christ's Authority	Luke 8:26–39	Luke 8:1–56
6	Believing in Jesus	Luke 9:18–27	Luke 9:1–10:42
7	Persistent Prayer	Luke 11:1–13	Luke 11:1–54
8	Trusting God	Luke 12:22–34	Luke 12:1–14:35
9	God's Love for People	Luke 15:11–32	Luke 15:1–18:43
10	True Worship	Luke 19:37–48	Luke 19:1–20:47
11	Christ's Sacrifice	Luke 23:26–49	Luke 21:1–23:56
12	Seeing Jesus	Luke 24:13–35	Luke 24:1–53

Six-Week Format

Week	Lessons Covered	Simplified Reading	Expanded Reading
1	Hope in God /Faith at Work	Luke 1:5–25; 5:17–26	Luke 1:1–5:39
2	A New Standard / Christ's Compassion	Luke 6:1–11; 7:11–23	Luke 6:1–7:50
3	Christ's Authority / Believing in Jesus	Luke 8:26–39; 9:18–27	Luke 8:1–10:42
4	Persistent Prayer / Trusting God	Luke 11:1–13; 12:22–34	Luke 11:1–14:35
5	God's Love for People /True Worship	Luke 15:11–32; 19:37–48	Luke 15:1–20:47
6	Christ's Sacrifice / Seeing Jesus	Luke 23:26–49; 24:13–35	Luke 21:1–24:53

Generally, the ideal size you will want for the group is between eight to ten people, which ensures everyone will have enough time to participate in discussions. If you have more people, you might want to break up the main group into smaller subgroups. Encourage those who show up at the first meeting to commit to attending the duration of the study, as this will help the group members get to know each other, create stability for the group, and help you know how to prepare each week.

Each of the lessons begins with a brief reflection that highlights the theme you will be discussing that week. As you begin your group time, have the group members briefly respond to the opening question to get them thinking about the topic at hand. Some people may want to tell a long story in response to one of these questions, but the goal is to keep the answers brief. Ideally, you want everyone in the group to get a chance to answer, so try to keep the responses to just a few minutes. If you have more talkative group members, say up front that everyone needs to limit his or her answer to two minutes.

Give the group members a chance to answer, but tell them to feel free to pass if they wish. With the rest of the study, it's generally not a good idea to have everyone answer every question—a free-flowing discussion is more desirable. But with the opening reflection question, you can go around the circle. Encourage shy people to share, but don't force them.

Before your first meeting, let the group members know how the lessons are broken down. During your group discussion time the members will be drawing on the answers they wrote to the Exploration and Reaction sections, so encourage them to always complete these ahead of time. Also, invite them to bring any questions and insights they uncovered while reading to your next meeting, especially if they had a breakthrough moment or if they didn't understand something they read.

WEEKLY PREPARATION

As the leader, there are a few things you should do to prepare for each meeting:

- *Read through the lesson.* This will help you to become familiar with the content and know how to structure the discussion times.
- *Decide which questions you want to discuss.* Depending on how you structure your group time, you may not be able to cover every question. So select the questions ahead of time that you absolutely want the group to explore.
- *Be familiar with the questions you want to discuss.* When the group meets you'll be watching the clock, so you want to make sure you are familiar with the Bible study questions you have selected. You can then spend time in the passage again when the group meets. In this way, you'll ensure you have the passage more deeply in your mind than your group members.
- *Pray for your group.* Pray for your group members throughout the week and ask God to lead them as they study his Word.
- *Bring extra supplies to your meeting.* The members should bring their own pens for writing notes, but it's a good idea to have extras available for those who forget. You may also want to bring paper and additional Bibles.

Note that in many cases there will not be one "right" answer to the question. Answers will vary, especially when the group members are being asked to share their personal experiences.

STRUCTURING THE DISCUSSION TIME

You will need to determine with your group how long you want to meet each week so you can plan your time accordingly. Generally, most groups like to meet for either sixty minutes or ninety minutes, so you could use one of the following schedules:

Section	60 Minutes	90 Minutes
WELCOME (members arrive and get settled)	5 minutes	10 minutes
REFLECTION (discuss the opening question for the lesson)	10 minutes	15 minutes
DISCUSSION (discuss the Bible study questions in the Exploration and Reaction sections)	35 minutes	50 minutes
PRAYER/CLOSING (pray together as a group and dismiss)	10 minutes	15 minutes

As the group leader, it is up to you to keep track of the time and keep things moving along according to your schedule. You might want to set a timer for each segment so both you and the group members know when your time is up. (Note that there are some good phone apps for timers that play a gentle chime or other pleasant sound instead of a disruptive noise.) Don't feel pressured to cover every question you have selected if the group has a good discussion going. Again, it's not necessary to go around the circle and make everyone share.

Don't be concerned if the group members are silent or slow to share. People are often quiet when they are pulling together their ideas, and this might be a new experience for them. Just ask a question and let it hang in the air until someone shares. You can then say, "Thank you. What about others? What came to you when you reflected on the passage?"

GROUP DYNAMICS

Leading a group through *Life Lessons from Luke* will prove to be highly rewarding both to you and your group members—but that doesn't mean you will not encounter any challenges along the way! Discussions can get off track. Group members may not be sensitive to the needs and ideas of others. Some might worry they will be expected to talk about matters that make them feel awkward. Others may express comments that result in disagreements. To help ease this strain on you and the group, consider the following ground rules:

- When someone raises a question or comment that is off the main topic, suggest you deal with it another time, or, if you feel led to go in that direction, let the group know you will be spending some time discussing it.
- If someone asks a question you don't know how to answer, admit it and move on. At your discretion, feel free to invite group members to comment on questions that call for personal experience.
- If you find one or two people are dominating the discussion time, direct a few questions to others in the group. Outside the main group time, ask the more dominating members to help you draw out the quieter ones. Work to make them a part of the solution instead of the problem.
- When a disagreement occurs, encourage the group members to process the matter in love. Encourage those on opposite sides to restate what they heard the other side say about the matter, and then invite each side to evaluate if that perception is accurate. Lead the group in examining other Scriptures related to the topic and look for common ground.

When any of these issues arise, encourage your group members to follow the words from the Bible: "Love one another" (John 13:34), "If it is possible, as far as it depends on you, live at peace with everyone" (Romans 12:18), and, "Be quick to listen, slow to speak and slow to become angry" (James 1:19).

Thank you again for taking the time to lead your group. May God reward your efforts and dedication and make your time together in this study fruitful for his kingdom.

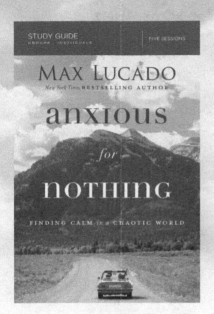
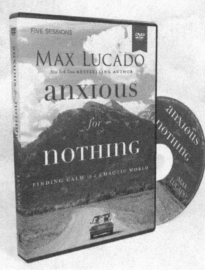

Inspired by what you just read?
Connect with Max.

Hope. Pure and simple.

Listen to Max's teaching ministry, UpWords, on the radio and online. Visit www.MaxLucado.com to get FREE resources for spiritual growth and encouragement, including:

• Archives of UpWords, Max's daily radio program, and a list of radio stations where it airs

• Devotionals and e-mails from Max

• First look at book excerpts

• Downloads of audio, video, and printed material

• Mobile content

You will also find an online store and special offers.

www.MaxLucado.com

1-800-822-9673

UpWords Ministries
P.O. Box 692170
San Antonio, TX 78269-2170

Join the Max Lucado community:

Follow Max on Twitter @MaxLucado
or at Facebook.com/MaxLucado